FOREWORD

The collection of "Everything Will Be Okay" travel phrasebooks published by T&P Books is designed for people traveling abroad for tourism and business. The phrasebooks contain what matters most - the essentials for basic communication. This is an indispensable set of phrases to "survive" while abroad.

This phrasebook will help you in most cases where you need to ask something, get directions, find out how much something costs, etc. It can also resolve difficult communication situations where gestures just won't help.

This book contains a lot of phrases that have been grouped according to the most relevant topics. You'll also find a mini dictionary with useful words - numbers, time, calendar, colors...

Take "Everything Will Be Okay" phrasebook with you on the road and you'll have an irreplaceable traveling companion who will help you find your way out of any situation and teach you to not fear speaking with foreigners.

TABLE OF CONTENTS

T&P Books Publishing

T&P Books Publishing

PHRASEBOOK

— BURMESE —

THE MOST IMPORTANT PHRASES

This phrasebook contains
the most important
phrases and questions
for basic communication
Everything you need
to survive overseas

By Andrey Taranov

T&P BOOKS

Phrasebook + 250-word dictionary

English-Burmese phrasebook & mini dictionary

By Andrey Taranov

The collection of "Everything Will Be Okay" travel phrasebooks published by T&P Books is designed for people traveling abroad for tourism and business. The phrasebooks contain what matters most - the essentials for basic communication. This is an indispensable set of phrases to "survive" while abroad.

You'll also find a mini dictionary with 250 useful words required for everyday communication - the names of months and days of the week, measurements, family members, and more.

T&P Books Publishing
www.tpbooks.com

ISBN: 978-1-83955-077-5

This book is also available in E-book formats.
Please visit www.tpbooks.com or the major online bookstores.

PRONUNCIATION

Transcription used in this book - the Myanmar Language Commission Transcription System (MLCTS)
A description of this system can be found here:
https://en.wiktionary.org/wiki/Wiktionary:Burmese_transliteration
https://en.wikipedia.org/wiki/MLC_Transcription_System

LIST OF ABBREVIATIONS

English abbreviations

ab.	-	about
adj	-	adjective
adv	-	adverb
anim.	-	animate
as adj	-	attributive noun used as adjective
e.g.	-	for example
etc.	-	et cetera
fam.	-	familiar
fem.	-	feminine
form.	-	formal
inanim.	-	inanimate
masc.	-	masculine
math	-	mathematics
mil.	-	military
n	-	noun
pl	-	plural
pron.	-	pronoun
sb	-	somebody
sing.	-	singular
sth	-	something
v aux	-	auxiliary verb
vi	-	intransitive verb
vi, vt	-	intransitive, transitive verb
vt	-	transitive verb

T&P BOOKS

BURMESE PHRASEBOOK

This section contains
important phrases that may
come in handy in various
real-life situations.
The phrasebook will help
you ask for directions, clarify
a price, buy tickets, and
order food at a restaurant

T&P Books Publishing

PHRASEBOOK
CONTENTS

T&P Books Publishing

The bare minimum

Excuse me, …

တစ်ဆိတ်လောက်ပါ...
ti' hsei' lau' pa…

Hello.

မင်္ဂလာပါ
min ga. la ba

Thank you.

ကျေးဇူးတင်ပါတယ်
kjei: zu: din ba de

Good bye.

နှုတ်ဆက်ပါတယ်
hnou' hse' pa de

Yes.

ဟုတ်ပါတယ်
hou' pa de

No.

မဟုတ်ပါဘူး
ma hou' pa bu:

I don't know.

ကျွန်ုပ်မသိပါဘူး
kjuhou' ma. dhi ba bu:

Where? | Where to? | When?

ဘယ်မှာလဲ | ဘယ်ကိုလဲ | ဘယ်တော့လဲ
be hma le: | be gou le: | be dau. le:

I need …

ကျွန်ုပ်...လိုအပ်တယ်
kjuhou'…lou a' te

I want …

ကျွန်ုပ်...လိုချင်တယ်
kjuhou'…lou gjin de

Do you have ...?

သင့်မှာ...ရှိပါလား
thin. hma…shi. ba dha. la:

Is there a … here?

ဒီမှာ...ရှိပါသလား
di hma…shi. ba dha la:

May I …?

ကျွန်ုပ်...လို့ရမလား
kjuhou'…lou. ja. ma. la:

…, please (polite request)

ကျေးဇူးပြု၍...
kjei: zu: pju. i….

I'm looking for …

ကျွန်ုပ်...ကိုရှာနေတာပါ
kjuhou' ... kou sha nei da. ba

the restroom

အိမ်သာ
ein dha

an ATM

အေတီအမ်စက်
ei ti. an se'

a pharmacy (drugstore)

ဆေးဆိုင်
hsei: zain

a hospital

ဆေးရုံ
hsei: joun

the police station

ရဲစခန်း
jè: za. gan:

the subway

မီသရို
mi' jou

---

a taxi	တက္ကစီ te' kasi
the train station	ရထားဘူတာရုံ jatha: buda joun

My name is …	ကျွန်ုပ်နာမည်ကတော့...ဖြစ်ပါတယ် kjunou' name ka. do….hpi' ba de
What's your name?	သင့်နာမည်ဘယ်လိုခေါ်ပါသလဲ thin. name be lou go ba dha la:
Could you please help me?	ကျေးဇူးပြု၍ ကျွန်ုပ်ကိုကူညီနိုင်မလား kjei: zu: pju. i. kjun p kou: ku nji nain ma. la:
I've got a problem.	ကျွန်ုပ်မှာအခက်အခဲရှိနေတယ် kjunou' hma akha' akhe: shi. nei de
I don't feel well.	ကျွန်ုပ်နေမကောင်းပါ kjunou' nei ma. kaun: ba
Call an ambulance!	လူနာတင်ကားခေါ်ပေးပါ lu na din ga: go bei: ba
May I make a call?	ကျွန်ုပ်ဖုန်းဆက်လို့ရမလား kjunou' hpoun: ze' lou. ja. ma. la:

I'm sorry.	တောင်းပန်ပါတယ် thaun: ban ba de
You're welcome.	ရပါတယ် ja. ba de

I, me	ကျွန်ုပ် kjunou'
you (inform.)	သင် thin
he	သူ thu
she	သူမ thu ma.
they (masc.)	သူတို့ thu dou.
they (fem.)	သူမတို့ thu ma. dou.
we	ကျွန်ုပ်တို့ kjunou' tou.
you (pl)	သင်တို့ thin dou.
you (sg, form.)	သင် thin

ENTRANCE	အဝင် awin
EXIT	အထွက် a htwe'
OUT OF ORDER	အလုပ်မလုပ်ပါ alou' ma lou' pa

CLOSED

ပိတ်သည်
pei' te

OPEN

ဖွင့်သည်
hpwin. de

FOR WOMEN

အမျိုးသမီးများအတွက်
amjou: dhami: mja: atwe'

FOR MEN

အမျိုးသားများအတွက်
amjou: dha: mja: atwe'

Questions

Where?
ဘယ်မှာလဲ
be hma le:

Where to?
ဘယ်ကိုလဲ
be gou le:

Where from?
ဘယ်ကလဲ
be ga. le:

Why?
ဘာကြောင့်လဲ
ba gjaun. le:

For what reason?
ဘာအတွက်ကြောင့်လဲ
ba atwe' kjaun. le:

When?
ဘယ်တော့လဲ
be do. le:

How long?
ဘယ်လောက်ကြာကြာလဲ
be lau' kja gja le:

At what time?
ဘယ်အချိန်မှာလဲ
be achein hma le:

How much?
ဘယ်လောက်ကျလဲ
be lau' kja le:

Do you have ...?
သင့်မှာ...ရှိပါသလား
thin. hma...shi. ba dha. la:

Where is ...?
...ဘယ်မှာရှိပါသလဲ
...be' hma shi. ba da le:

What time is it?
ဘယ်အချိန်ရှိပြီလဲ
be achein shi. bja le:

May I make a call?
ကျွန်ုပ်ဖုန်းဆက်လို့ရမလား
kjunou' hpoun: ze' lou. ja. ma. la:

Who's there?
ဘယ်သူလဲ
be dhu le:

Can I smoke here?
ကျွန်ုပ်ဒီမှာ ဆေးလိပ်သောက်လို့ရမလား
kjunou' di hma zei: lei' thau' lou. ja ma la:

May I ...?
ကျွန်ုပ်...လို့ရမလား
kjunou'...lou. ja. ma. la:

Needs

I'd like …	ကျွန်ုပ်...လိုချင်တယ် kjuhou'…lou gjin de
I don't want …	ကျွန်ုပ် မ...ချင်ဘူး kjuhou' ma....chin bu:
I'm thirsty.	ကျွန်ုပ်ရေဆာတယ် kjuhou' jei za de
I want to sleep.	ကျွန်ုပ်အိပ်ချင်တယ် kjuhou' ei' chin de

I want …	ကျွန်ုပ်...လိုချင်တယ် kjuhou'…lou gjin de
to wash up	ကိုယ်လက်သန့်စင် kou le' than. zin
to brush my teeth	သွားတိုက် thwa: tai'
to rest a while	ခဏအနားယူ khana. ana: ju
to change my clothes	အဝတ်လဲ awu' le:

to go back to the hotel	ဟော်တယ်ကိုပြန် ho te kou bin
to buy …	...ဝယ် …we
to go to …	...သို့သွား …thou. dhwa:
to visit …	အလည်သွား ale dhwa:
to meet with …	...နှင့်တွေ့ …hnin. dwei.
to make a call	ဖုန်းခေါ် hpoun: go

I'm tired.	ကျွန်ုပ်ပင်ပန်းနေတယ် kjuhou' pin ban nei de
We are tired.	ကျွန်ုပ်တို့ပင်ပန်းနေကြပြီ kjuhou' tou. bin ban: nei gja bji
I'm cold.	ကျွန်ုပ်အေးတယ် kjuhou' ei: de
I'm hot.	ကျွန်ုပ်ပူတယ် kjuhou' pu de
I'm OK.	ကျွန်ုပ်အဆင်ပြေပါတယ် kjuhou' ahsin pjei ba de

I need to make a call.

ကျွန်ုပ်ဖုန်းဆက်ဖို့လိုတယ်
kjuhou' hpoun: ze' hpou. lou de

I need to go to the restroom.

ကျွန်ုပ်အိမ်သာသွားဖို့လိုတယ်
kjuhou' ein dha dhwa: hpou. lou de

I have to go.

ကျွန်ုပ်သွားရတော့မယ်
kjuhou' thwa: ja. do. me

I have to go now.

ကျွန်ုပ်သွားဖို့လိုတယ်
kjuhou' thwa: bou. lou de

Asking for directions

Excuse me, …	တစ်ဆိတ်လောက်ပါ... ti' hsei' lau' pa…
Where is …?	...ဘယ်မှာရှိပါသလဲ …be' hma shi. ba da le:
Which way is …?	...ဘယ်ဘက်မှာရှိပါသလဲ …be' be' hma shi. ba da le:
Could you help me, please?	ကျေးဇူးပြု၍ ကျွန်ုပ်ကိုကူညီလို့ရမလား kjei: zu: pju. i. kjun p kou: ku nji lou. ja. ma. la:
I'm looking for …	ကျွန်ုပ်...ကိုရှာနေတာပါ kjuhou' … kou sha nei da. ba
I'm looking for the exit.	ကျွန်ုပ်ထွက်ပေါက်ကိုရှာနေတာပါ kjuhou' hte' pau' kou sha nei da ba
I'm going to …	ကျွန်ုပ်...ကိုသွားနေတာပါ kjuhou'…kou dhwa: nei da ba
Am I going the right way to …?	ကျွန်ုပ်...ကိုသွားနေတာမှန်ရဲ့ လား kjuhou'…kou dhwa: nei da hman je. la:
Is it far?	အဲ့ဒါဝေးလား e. da wei: la:
Can I get there on foot?	ကျွန်ုပ်အဲ့ဒီကိုလမ်းလျှောက်သွား လို့ရပါသလား kjuhou' e. di gou lan: shau' dhwa: lou. ja. ba dha. la:
Can you show me on the map?	ကျေးဇူးပြု၍ ကျွန်ုပ်ကိုမြေပုံပေါ်မှာ ပြပေးပါလား kjei: zu: pju. i. kjun p kou:
Show me where we are right now.	ကျေးဇူးပြု၍ ကျွန်ုပ်တို့အခု ဘယ်မှာလဲဆိုတာ ပြပေးပါ kjei: zu: pju. i. kjun p tou. akhou. be hma le: zou da pja bei: ba
Here	ဒီမှာပါ di hma ba
There	အဲ့ဒီမှာ e. di hma
This way	ဒီဘက်ကို di be' kou
Turn right.	ညာဘက်ကိုကွေ့ ပါ nja be' kou gwei. ba
Turn left.	ဘယ်ဘက်ကိုကွေ့ပါ be be' kou gwei. ba

first (second, third) turn

ပထမ (ဒုတိယ၊ တတိယ) အကွေ့
pahtama. (du. ti. ja./ ta. ti. ja.) akwe.

to the right

ညာဘက်ကို
ŋa be' kou

to the left

ဘယ်ဘက်ကို
be be' kou

Go straight ahead.

တည့်တည့်သွားပါ
te. de. dhwa: ba

Signs

WELCOME!	ကြိုဆိုပါ၏
	kjou zou ba i
ENTRANCE	အဝင်
	awin
EXIT	အထွက်
	a htwe'
PUSH	တွန်းပါ
	tun: ba
PULL	ဆွဲပါ
	hswe: ba
OPEN	ဖွင့်သည်
	hpwin. de
CLOSED	ပိတ်သည်
	pei' te
FOR WOMEN	အမျိုးသမီးများအတွက်
	amjou: dhami: mja: atwe'
FOR MEN	အမျိုးသားများအတွက်
	amjou: dha: mja: atwe'
GENTLEMEN, GENTS	ကျား
	kja:
WOMEN	မ
	ma.
DISCOUNTS	လျှော့ဈေး
	sho. zei:
SALE	လျှော့ဈေး
	sho. zei:
FREE	အခမဲ့
	akha me.
NEW!	အသစ်စက်စက်
	athi' se' se'
ATTENTION!	သတိ
	thadi.
NO VACANCIES	နေရာလွတ်မရှိ
	nei ja lwa' ma. shi.
RESERVED	ကြိုတင်မှာယူထားပြီး
	kjou din hma ju da: pji:
ADMINISTRATION	အုပ်ချုပ်ရေး
	ou' chu' jei:
STAFF ONLY	ဝန်ထမ်းသီးသန့်
	wun dan: dhi: dhan.

BEWARE OF THE DOG!   သတိ၊ ခွေးကိုက်တတ်သည်
thadi./ khwei: gou' ta' te

NO SMOKING!   ဆေးလိပ်မသောက်ရ
hsei: lei' ma. dhau' ja.

DO NOT TOUCH!   မထိရ
ma. di. ja.

DANGEROUS   အန္တရာယ်
an dare

DANGER   အန္တရာယ်
an dare

HIGH VOLTAGE   ဗို့အားပြင်းသည်
bou. a: bjin: de

NO SWIMMING!   ရေမကူးရ
jei ma. gu: ja.

OUT OF ORDER   အလုပ်မလုပ်ပါ
alou' ma lou' pa

FLAMMABLE   မီးလောင်လွယ်သည်
mi: laun lwe de

FORBIDDEN   တားမြစ်ထားသည်
ta: mji' hta: te

NO TRESPASSING!   မကျူးကျော်ရ
ma. gju: gjo ja

WET PAINT   ဆေးစိုနေသည်
hsei: zou nei de

CLOSED FOR RENOVATIONS   ပြုပြင်ရန်ပိတ်ထားသည်
pju: bjin jan bei' hta: de

WORKS AHEAD   ရှေ့တွင် လမ်းပြင်နေသည်
shei. dwin lan: bjin nei de

DETOUR   လမ်းလွှဲ
lan: hlwe:

19

Transportation. General phrases

plane	လေယာဉ် lei jan
train	ရထား jàtha:
bus	ဘတ်စ်ကား ba's ka:
ferry	ဖယ်ရီ hpe jì
taxi	တက္ကစီ te' kasi
car	မော်တော်ကား mo to ka:
schedule	အချိန်ဇယား achein zaja:
Where can I see the schedule?	အချိန်ဇယား ဘယ်မှာကြည့်လို့ရပါသလဲ achein zaja: be' hma kji. lou. ja. ba da le:
workdays (weekdays)	ရုံးဖွင့်ရက် joun: hpwin je'
weekends	ရုံးပိတ်ရက် joun: bei' je'
holidays	အားလပ်ရက် a: la' je'
DEPARTURE	ထွက်ခွါခြင်း htwe' khwa gjin:
ARRIVAL	ဆိုက်ရောက်ခြင်း hseu' jau' chin
DELAYED	နောက်ကျသည် nau' kja. de
CANCELLED	ပယ်ဖျက်သည် pe hpje' te
next (train, etc.)	နောက် nau'
first	ပထမ pahtama.
last	နောက်ဆုံး nau' hsoun:
When is the next ...?	နောက်...ကဘယ်အချိန်လဲ nau'...ka. be achein le:
When is the last ...?	နောက်ဆုံး...ကဘယ်အချိန်ထွက်မှာလဲ nau' hsoun:...ka. be achein dwe' hma le:

When is the first ...?

ပထမဆုံး...ကဘယ်
အချိန်ထွက်မှာလဲ
pahtama. zoun:...ka be
achein dwe' hma le:

transfer (change of trains, etc.)

ပြောင်းစီးခြင်း
pjaun: zi: gjin:

to make a transfer

ပြောင်းစီးသည်
pjaun: zi: de

Do I need to make a transfer?

ကျွန်ုပ်ပြောင်းစီးဖို့လိုပါသလား
kjuhou pjaun: zi: hpou. lou ba de

Buying tickets

Where can I buy tickets?	လက်မှတ်ဘယ်မှာဝယ်လို့ရပါသလဲ le' hma' be hma lou. ja. ba dha. le:
ticket	လက်မှတ် le' hma'
to buy a ticket	လက်မှတ်ဝယ်သည် le' hma' we de
ticket price	လက်မှတ်ဖိုး le' hma' hpou:

Where to?	ဘယ်ကိုလဲ be gou le:
To what station?	ဘယ်ဘူတာအထိလဲ be bu da ahti le:
I need ...	ကျွန်ုပ်....လိုအပ်တယ် kjunou'...lou a' te
one ticket	လက်မှတ်တစ်စောင် le' hma' ti' sain
two tickets	လက်မှတ်နှစ်စောင် le' hma' hni' sain
three tickets	လက်မှတ်သုံးစောင် le' hma' thoun: zain

one-way	တစ်လမ်းတည်း ti' lan: de:
round-trip	အသွား/အပြန်ခရီး athwa:/apjan gaji:
first class	ပထမတန်း pahtama. dan:
second class	ဒုတိယတန်း du. di. ja. dan:

today	ဒီနေ့ di nei.
tomorrow	မနက်ဖြန် mane bjan
the day after tomorrow	သသဘက်ခါ dhabe' kha
in the morning	မနက်မှာ mane' hma
in the afternoon	နေ့လယ်မှာ nei. le hma
in the evening	ညနေမှာ nja. nei hma

aisle seat	လူသွားလမ်းနဲ့ကပ်လျက်နေရာ lu dhwa: lan: ne. ga' lje' nei ja
window seat	ပြတင်းပေါက်နဲ့ကပ်လျက်နေရာ badin: pau' ne. ka' lje' nei ja
How much?	ဘယ်လောက်လဲ be lau' le:
Can I pay by credit card?	ခရက်ဒစ်ကဒ်နဲ့ရှင်းလို့ရပါသလား kha. je' di' ka' he. shin: lou. ja. ba dha. la:

Bus

bus	ဘတ်စ်ကား ba's ka:
intercity bus	အခြားမြို့သွားဘတ်စ်ကား apja: mjou. dhwa: ba's ka:
bus stop	ဘတ်စ်ကားမှတ်တိုင် ba's ka: hmat tain
Where's the nearest bus stop?	အနီးဆုံးဘတ်စ်ကား မှတ်တိုင်ဘယ်နားမှာလဲ ani: zoun: be's ka: hma' dain be na: hma le:

number (bus ~, etc.)	နံပါတ် nan ba'
Which bus do I take to get to …?	…ကိုရောက်ဖို့ဘယ်ဘတ်စ်ကား ကိုကျွန်ုပ်စီးရပါမလဲ …kou jau' phou. be ba' s ka: kou kjwan b si: ja ba ma le:
Does this bus go to …?	ဒီဘတ်စကားက…အထိသွားပါသလား di ba' za. ga: ca….ahti. dwa: ba dha la:
How frequent are the buses?	ဘတ်စ်ကားတွေဘယ်လောက်ကြား ပြီးလာပါသလဲ ba's ka: twei de lau' khja pja la ba da le:

every 15 minutes	၁၅ မိနစ်ခြား ta' hse. nga: mi ni' cha:
every half hour	နာရီဝက်ခြား na ji we chin
every hour	တစ်နာရီခြား ti' na ji gja:
several times a day	တစ်နေ့ကိုအကြိမ်တော်တော်များများ ti' nei gou achein to do mja: mja:
… times a day	တစ်နေ့…ကြိမ် ti' nei….kein

schedule	အချိန်ဇယား achein zaja:
Where can I see the schedule?	အချိန်ဇယား ဘယ်မှာကြည့်လို့ရပါသလဲ achein zaja: be' hma kji. lou. ja. ba da le:
When is the next bus?	နောက်ဘတ်စ်ကားကဘယ်အချိန်လဲ nau' ba's ka: dhe achein le:
When is the first bus?	ပထမဆုံးဘတ်စ်ကားက ဘယ်အချိန်ထွက်ပါသလဲ pahtama. zoun: ba's ka: ga. …be achein dwe' ba dha. le:

When is the last bus?

နောက်ဆုံးဘတ်စ်ကားကာ
ဘယ်အချိန်ထွက်ပါသလဲ
nau' hsoun: ba's ka: ga.
be achein dwe' ba dha. le:

stop

မှတ်တိုင်
hma' tain

next stop

နောက်မှတ်တိုင်
nau' hma' tain

last stop (terminus)

နောက်ဆုံးမှတ်တိုင်
nau' hsoun: hma' tain

Stop here, please.

ကျေးဇူးပြု၍ ဒီမှာရပ်ပေးပါ
kjei: zu: pju. i. di hma ja' pei: ba

Excuse me, this is my stop.

ခွင့်ပြုပါ၊ ဒါကျွန်ုပ်ဆင်း
ရမယ့်မှတ်တိုင်ပါ
khwin. bju. ba/ da kjun p hsin:
jame hma' tain ba

Train

train	ရထား játha:
suburban train	မြို့ပတ်ရထား mjou. ba' ja da:
long-distance train	အဝေးပြေးရထား awei: bjei: ja. da:
train station	ရထားဘူတာရုံ játha: buda joun
Excuse me, where is the exit to the platform?	တစ်ဆိတ်လျှောက်၊ ရထားစင်္ကြံဆီသွား တဲ့ထွက်ပေါက်ကဘယ်မှာလဲ ti' hsei' lau'/ jahta: zin gjan zi dhwa: de dwe' bau' ka. be hma le:

Does this train go to …?	ဒီရထားက... အထိသွားပါသလား di ja hta: ga….ahti. dhwa: ba dha la:
next train	နောက်ရထား náu' jada:
When is the next train?	နောက်ရထားက ဘယ်အချိန်ပါလဲ náu' jada: ga. be achein ba le:
Where can I see the schedule?	အချိန်ဇယား ဘယ်မှာကြည့်လို့ရပါသလဲ achein zaja: be' hma kji. lou'. ja. ba da le:
From which platform?	ဘယ်စင်္ကြံကပါလဲ be zin: gjan ka. ba le:
When does the train arrive in …?	ရထားက...ကိုဘယ်အချိန်ရောက်မှာလဲ játha: ga….kou be achein jau' hma le:

Please help me.	ကျေးဇူးပြု၍ ကျွန်ုပ်ကိုကူညီပါ kjei: zu: pju. i. kjun p kou gu nji ba
I'm looking for my seat.	ကျွန်ုပ်နေရာကိုရှာနေတာပါ kjúhou' nei já kou sha nei da ba
We're looking for our seats.	ကျွန်ုပ်တို့နေရာတွေကိုရှာနေတာပါ kjúhou' tou. nei já dwe kou sha nei da ba
My seat is taken.	ကျွန်ုပ်နေရာက မအားတော့ဘူး kjúhou' nei ja ga. ma. a: dó. bu:
Our seats are taken.	ကျွန်ုပ်တို့နေရာတွေက မအားတော့ဘူး kjúhou' tou. nei já dwe ga. ma. a: do. bu:

I'm sorry but this is my seat.	တစ်ဆိတ်လောက် ဒါကကျွန်ုပ်နေရာပါ ti' hsei lau' da ga. gjwina' nei já ba
Is this seat taken?	ဒီနေရာ အားပါသလား di nei ja a: ba dha le:
May I sit here?	ဒီမှာထိုင်လို့ ရပါသလား di hma dain lou. ja. ba dha la:

On the train. Dialogue (No ticket)

Ticket, please.
ကျေးဇူးပြု၍ သင့်ရဲ့လက်မှတ်ပြပါ
kjei: zu: pju. i. thin. je. le' hma' pja ba

I don't have a ticket.
ကျွန်ုပ်မှာ လက်မှတ်မရှိပါဘူး
kjunou' hma le' hma' ma. shi. ba bu:

I lost my ticket.
ကျွန်ုပ်လက်မှတ် ပျောက်သွားလို့ပါ
kjunou' le' hma' pjau' thwa: lou. ba

I forgot my ticket at home.
ကျွန်ုပ်လက်မှတ်
အိမ်မှာမေ့ကျန်ခဲ့လို့ပါ
kjunou' le' hma'
ein' hma mei. kjan ge. lou. ba

You can buy a ticket from me.
ကျွန်ုပ်ဆီမှာ
သိင်လက်မှတ်ဝယ်လို့ရပါတယ်
kjunou' his hma
thin le' hma' we lou. ja. ba de

You will also have to pay a fine.
မင်းဒဏ်ငွေဆောင်ရလိမ့်မယ်
min: dan ngwei zaun ja. lein. me

Okay.
ကောင်းပါပြီ
kaun: ba bji

Where are you going?
ဘယ်ကိုသွားနေတာလဲ
be gou dhwa: nei da le:

I'm going to …
ကျွန်ုပ်…ကိုသွားနေတာပါ
kjunou'…kou dhwa: nei da ba

How much? I don't understand.
ဘယ်လောက်လဲ၊ ကျွန်ုပ်နားမလည်လို့ပါ
be lau' le:/ kjanap na: ma. le dhua. ba

Write it down, please.
ကျေးဇူးပြု၍ ရေးပေးပါ
kjei: zu: pju. i. jei: bei: ba

Okay. Can I pay with a credit card?
ဟုတ်ကဲ့၊ ကျွန်တော်ခရက်ဒစ်ကဒ်နဲ့ရှင်း
လို့ရပါသလား
hou' ke./ kjun do gaje' di' ka' ne. shin:
lou. ja. ba dha. ala:

Yes, you can.
ဟုတ်ကဲ့၊ ရပါတယ်
hou' ke./ ja ba de

Here's your receipt.
ဒီမှာသင့်ရဲ့ ပြေစာပါ
di hma dhin. jei. pjei za ba

Sorry about the fine.
ဒဏ်ငွေအတွက်စိတ်မကောင်းဘူး
dan ngwei atwe' si' ma. gaun: ba bu:

That's okay. It was my fault.
ရပါတယ်၊ ဒါကကျွန်ုပ်အမှားပါ
ja. ba de/ da ga gjun p ahma: ba

Enjoy your trip.
ပျော်ရွှင်ဖွယ်ခရီးဖြစ်ပါစေ
pjo shin bwe: khaji: hpji' ba zei

Taxi

taxi	**တက္ကစီ** te' kasi
taxi driver	**တက္ကစီမောင်းသူ** te' kasi maun: dhu
to catch a taxi	**တက္ကစီငှါးသည်** te' kasi hnga: de
taxi stand	**တက္ကစီဂိတ်** te' kasi gei'
Where can I get a taxi?	**ကျွန်ုပ် တက္ကစီဘယ်မှာငှါး လို့ရပါမလဲ** kjunou' ta' ka. si be hma hnga: lou. ja ba ma. la:
to call a taxi	**တက္ကစီခေါ်သည်** te' kasi go de
I need a taxi.	**ကျွန်ုပ်တက္ကစီလိုသည်** kjunou' ti' ka si lou de
Right now.	**အခုချက်ချင်းပါ** akhu che' chin: ba
What is your address (location)?	**သင့်ရဲ့လိပ်စာကဘာပါလဲ** thin. je. lei' sa ga. ba ba le:
My address is ...	**ကျွန်ုပ်လိပ်စာက...** kjunou' lei' sa ga....
Your destination?	**ဘယ်ကိုသွားမှာလဲ** be gou dhwa: hma le:
Excuse me, ...	**တစ်ဆိတ်လောက်ပါ...** ti' hsei' lau' pa...
Are you available?	**တက္ကစီအားပါသလား** te' kasi a: ba dha. la:
How much is it to get to ...?	**...အထိဘယ်လောက်ကျပါသလဲ** ...ahti be lau' kja. ba da le:
Do you know where it is?	**ဒါကဘယ်မှာလဲဆိုတာ သင်သိပါသလား** da ga. be hma. le: zou da dhin dhi. ba dha la:
Airport, please.	**ကျေးဇူးပြု၍ လေဆိပ်ကိုပို့ပေးပါ** kjei: zu: pju. i. lei hsei' kou bou. bei: ba
Stop here, please.	**ကျေးဇူးပြု၍ ဒီမှာရပ်ပေးပါ** kjei: zu: pju. i. di hma ja' pei: ba
It's not here.	**ဒီမှာမဟုတ်ပါဘူး** di hma hou' ba dhu:

This is the wrong address.	လိပ်စာမှားနေပါတယ်
	lei' sa hma: nei ba de
Turn left.	အခုဘယ်ဘက်ကိုပါ
	akhu. be' be' kau ba
Turn right.	အခုညာဘက်ကိုပါ
	akhu. nja' be' kau ba

How much do I owe you?	ဘယ်လောက်ပေးရပါမလဲ
	be lau' pei: ja ba le:
I'd like a receipt, please.	ကျေးဇူးပြု၍ ချက်ပြန်ပေးပါ
	kjei: zu: pju. i. che' pjan bei: ba
Keep the change.	အကြွေမအမ်းပါတော့နဲ့
	akjwei ma. an: ba do. ne.

Would you please wait for me?	ကျေးဇူးပြု၍ ကျွန်ုပ်ကိုစောင့်ပေးပါ
	kjei: zu: pju. i. kjun p kou: zaun. bei: ba
five minutes	ငါးမိနစ်
	nga: mi. ni'
ten minutes	ဆယ်မိနစ်
	hse mi. ni'
fifteen minutes	ဆယ့်ငါးမိနစ်
	hse. nga: mi. ni'
twenty minutes	မိနစ်နှစ်ဆယ်
	mi. ni' hni' ze
half an hour	နာရီဝက်
	na ji we'

Hotel

Hello.	မင်္ဂလာပါ min ga. la ba
My name is …	ကျွန်ုပ်နာမည်ကတော့...ဖြစ်ပါတယ် kjuhou' name ka. do....hpi' ba de
I have a reservation.	ကျွန်ုပ်ကြိုတင်မှာထားပြီးပြီ kjuhou' kjou din hma hta: pji: pji
I need …	ကျွန်ုပ်....လိုအပ်တယ် kjuhou'...lou a' te
a single room	တစ်ယောက်ခန်း ti' jau' khan:
a double room	နှစ်ယောက်ခန်း hni' jau' khah:
How much is that?	ဘယ်လောက်ကျပါသလဲ be lau' kja ba dha le:
That's a bit expensive.	ဒါကနည်းနည်းတော့ဈေးများပါတယ် da ga. ne: do. zei: mja: ba de
Do you have anything else?	သင့်တို့မှာနောက်ထပ်တစ်ခုခုများ ရှိပါသေးသလား thin dou. hma: nau' hta' ti' khu. gu. gja: shi. ba dhei: dha la:
I'll take it.	ကျွန်ုပ် ဒါကို ယူပါမယ် kjuhou' da gou ju ba me
I'll pay in cash.	ကျွန်ုပ်လက်ငင်းပဲရှင်းပါမယ် kjuhou' le' ngin: be: hmin: ba. me
I've got a problem.	ကျွန်ုပ်မှာအခက်အခဲရှိနေတယ် kjuhou' hma akha' akhe: shi. nei de
My … is broken.	ကျွန်ုပ်ရဲ့ ...ကျိုးသွားလို့ပါ kjuhou' je....kjou: thwa: lou. ba
My … is out of order.	ကျွန်ုပ်ရဲ့ ...ကအလုပ် မလုပ်တော့လို့ပါ kjuhou' je....ka. alou' ma. lou' to. lou. ba
TV	တီဗီ ti bi
air conditioner	အဲကွန်း e kun:
tap	ရေပိုက်ခေါင်း jei bai' khaun:
shower	ရေပန်း jei ban:
sink	ဘေစင် bei zin

safe	မီးခံသေတ္တာ mi: gan dhi' ta
door lock	သော့ခလောက် tho. ga. lau'
electrical outlet	ပလပ်ပေါက် pa. la' pau'
hairdryer	ဒရိုင်ယာ da. jain ja

I don't have …	ကျွန်ုပ်မှာ…မရှိပါဘူး kjunou' hma…ma. shi. ba bu:
water	ရေ jei
light	မီး mi:
electricity	လျှပ်စစ် hlja' si'

Can you give me …?	ကျွန်ုပ်ကို…ပေးလို့ရမလား kjunou' kou…pei: lou. ja. ma. la:
a towel	တဘက် tabe'
a blanket	စောင် saun
slippers	စလစ်ပါ sali' pa
a robe	ရေလဲဝတ်စုံ jei le: wu' zoun
shampoo	ခေါင်းလျှော်ရည် gaun: sho je
soap	ဆပ်ပြာ hsa' pja

I'd like to change rooms.	ကျွန်ုပ်အခန်းပြောင်းချင်ပါတယ် kjunou' akhan: pjaun: chin ba de
I can't find my key.	ကျွန်ုပ်ရဲ့သော့ရှာမတွေ့တော့လို့ပါ kjunou' je. dho. sha ma. dwei. do. lou. ba
Could you open my room, please?	ကျေးဇူးပြု၍ ကျွန်ုပ်ရဲ့အခန်း ကိုဖွင့်ပေးပါ kjei: zu: pju. i. kjun p je. akhan: kou bei: ba

Who's there?	ဘယ်သူလဲ be dhu le:
Come in!	ဝင်ခဲ့ပါ win ge. ba
Just a minute!	တစ်မိနစ်လောက်ပါ ti' mi hni' lau' pa
Not right now, please.	ကျေးဇူးပြု၍ အခုမဟုတ်သေးပါဘူး kjei: zu: pju. i. akhu. ma. hou' thei: ba dhu:

Come to my room, please.

ကျေးဇူးပြု၍ ကျွန်ုပ်အခီဝင်ခဲ့ပါ
kjei: zu: pju. i. kjun p his win ge. ba

I'd like to order food service.

ကျွန်ုပ်အခန်းတို့ စားစရာ
မှာချင်ပါတယ်
kjunou' akhan: kou za: zaja
hma chin ba de

My room number is …

ကျွန်ုပ်ရဲ့ အခန်းနံပါတ်ကဓ
တို့....ဖြစ်ပါတယ်
kjunou' je. akhan: nan ba
t ka do....hpji' ba de

I'm leaving …

ကျွန်ုပ် ပြန်ပါတော့မယ်
kjunou' pjan ba do. me

We're leaving …

ကျွန်ုပ်တို့ ပြန်ပါတော့မယ်
kjunou' tou. bjan ga do. me

right now

အခု
akhu.

this afternoon

ဒီနေ့နေလယ်စာစားချိန်ပြီးနောက်
di nei. le za za: gjin bji: nau'

tonight

ဒီနေ့ညနေ
di nei. nja nei

tomorrow

မနက်ဖြန်
mane bjan

tomorrow morning

မနက်ဖြန်မနက်
mane bjan mane'

tomorrow evening

မနက်ဖြန်ညနေ
mane bjan nja. nei

the day after tomorrow

သသဘက်ခါ
dhabe' kha

I'd like to pay.

ကျွန်ုပ် ပိုက်ဆံရှင်းချင်ပါတယ်
kjunou' pou' hsan shin: chin ba de

Everything was wonderful.

အားလုံး အရမ်းကောင်းခဲ့ပါတယ်
a: louh: ayan: kaun: ge. ba de

Where can I get a taxi?

ကျွန်ုပ် တက္ကစီဘယ်မှာငှား
လို့ရပါမလဲ
kjunou' ta' ka. si be hma hnga:
lou. ja ba ma. la:

Would you call a taxi for me, please?

ကျေးဇူးပြု၍
ကျွန်ုပ်ကိုတက္ကစီခေါ် ပေးပါ
kjei: zu: pju.
i. kjun p kou: te' ka si kho bei: ba

Restaurant

Can I look at the menu, please?
ကျေးဇူးပြု၍ သင်တို့ရဲ့ မီညူးကို
ကြည့်လို့ရမလား
kjei: zu: pju. i. thin. dou. je. mi nju: gou
kji. lou. ja. ma. la:

Table for one.
တစ်ယောက်ဝိုင်း
ti' jau' wain:

There are two (three, four) of us.
ကျွန်ုပ်တို့က နှစ်ယောက်
(သုံးယောက်/ လေးယောက်) ပါ
kjunou' tou. ga hni' jau'
(thaun: jau'/ lei: jau')

Smoking
ဆေးလိပ်သောက်နိုင်သော
hsei: lei' ma. dhau' nain. de.

No smoking
ဆေးလိပ်မသောက်ရသော
hsei: lei' ma. dhau' ja.de.

Excuse me! (addressing a waiter)
တစ်ဆိတ်လောက်ပါ
ti' hsei' lau' pa

menu
မီညူး
mi nju:

wine list
ဝိုင်စာရင်း
wain za jin:

The menu, please.
ကျေးဇူးပြု၍ မီညူးပေးပါ
kjei: zu: pju. i. mi nju: bei: ba

Are you ready to order?
မှာလို့ရပါပြီလား
hma lou. ja. ba bji la:

What will you have?
ဘာမှာချင်ပါသလဲ
ba hma gjain ba da le:

I'll have …
ကျွန်ုပ်…ပါမယ်
kjunou'…pa me

I'm a vegetarian.
ကျွန်ုပ်ကသက်သက်လွတ်သမားပါ
kjunou' ka dhe' dhe' lwa' dha. ma: ba

meat
အသား
atha:

fish
ငါး
nga:

vegetables
အသီးအရွက်
athi: ajwe'

Do you have vegetarian dishes?
အသီးအရွက်ဟင်းတွေရှိပါသလား
athi: ajwe' hin: shi. ba dha la:

I don't eat pork.
ကျွန်ုပ်ဝက်သားမစားပါဘူး
kjunou' we' tha: ma. za: ba dhu:

He /she/ doesn't eat meat.

သူ/သူမ/ ကအသားမစားပါဘူး
thu / thu ma./ ka. atha: ma. za: ba bu:

I am allergic to …

ကျွန်ုပ်က…နဲ့မတည့်ပါဘူး
kjuhou' ka:….ne. ma. de. ba dhu:

Would you please bring me …

ကျေးဇူးပြု၍ ကျွန်ုပ်ကို…ယူခဲ့ပေးပါ
kjei: zu: pju. i. kjun p
kou…yuuqee•pe:páa

salt | pepper | sugar

ဆား | ငရုတ်သီး | သကြား
hsa: | nga. jou' dhi: | thakja:

coffee | tea | dessert

ကော်ဖီ | လဘက်ရည် | အချိုပွဲ
ko hpi | la be' ji | achou bwe:

water | sparkling | plain

ရေ | ဂက်စ်ပါသော | ဂက်စ်မပါသော
jei | ga's pa de. | ga's ma. ba de.

a spoon | fork | knife

ဇွန်း | ခက်ရင်း | ဓား
zun: | khe jin: | da:

a plate | napkin

ပန်းကန်ပြား | တစ်ရှူး
bagan: bja: | ti' shju:

Enjoy your meal!

စားကောင်းပါစေ
sa: gaun: ba zei

One more, please.

ကျေးဇူးပြု၍နောက်ထပ်တစ်ခု
ထပ်ယူခဲ့ပေးပါ
kjei: zu: pju. i. nau' ti' hta' khou
hta' ju ge. bei: ba

It was very delicious.

အရမ်းအရသာရှိခဲ့ပါတယ်
ajan: aja dha shi. khe. ba de

check | change | tip

ချက် | အကြွေ | ဘောက်စူး
che' | akjwei | bau' su:

Check, please.
(Could I have the check, please?)

ကျေးဇူးပြု၍ ချက်ပေးပါ
kjei: zu: pju. i. che' bei: ba

Can I pay by credit card?

ခရက်ဒစ်ကဒ်နဲ့ရှင်းလို့ရပါသလား
kha. je' di' ka' ne. shin: lou. ja. ba dha. la:

I'm sorry, there's a mistake here.

တစ်ဆိတ်လောက်ပါ၊ ဒီမှာမှားနေပါတယ်
ti' hsei' lau' pa/ di hma hma: nei ba de

Shopping

Can I help you?	ကူညီပေးလို့ရမလား ku nji bei: lou. ja. ma. la:
Do you have …?	သင့်မှာ…ရှိပါသလား thin.' hma…shi. ba dha. la:
I'm looking for …	ကျွန်ုပ်…ကိုရှာနေတာပါ kjunou' … kou sha nei da. ba
I need …	ကျွန်ုပ်….လိုအပ်တယ် kjunou'…lou a' te
I'm just looking.	ကျွန်ုပ်ဒီအတိုင်းလိုက်ကြည့်တာပါ kjunou' di atain.' lai' gji. ta ba
We're just looking.	ကျွန်ုပ်တို့ဒီအတိုင်းလိုက်ကြည့်ကြတာပါ kjunou' tou. atein.' lou' kji. kja. da ba
I'll come back later.	ကျွန်ုပ်နောက်မှထပ်လာခဲ့ပါမယ် kjunou' nau' hma. da' la ge. ba me:
We'll come back later.	ကျွန်ုပ်တို့နောက်မှထပ်လာခဲ့ ကြပါမယ် kjunou' tou nau' hma. da' la ge. gja. ba me
discounts | sale	လျှော့ဈေး | ရောင်းဈေး sho. zei: | jaun: zei:
Would you please show me …	ကျေးဇူးပြု၍ ကျွန်ုပ်ကို…ပြပါ kjei: zu: pju. i. kjun p kou…pja: ba
Would you please give me …	ကျေးဇူးပြု၍ ကျွန်ုပ်ကို…ပေးပါ kjei: zu: pju. i. kjun p kou…pei: ba
Can I try it on?	ကျွန်ုပ် ဒါကို ဝတ်ကြည့်လို့ရပါသလား kjunou' dã gou wu' kji. lou. ja. ba dha la:
Excuse me, where's the fitting room?	တစ်ဆိတ်လောက်ပါ/ အဝတ်လဲခန်းဘယ်မှာရှိပါသလဲ ti' hsei' lau' pa/ awu' le: gan: be hma shi ba dha. le:
Which color would you like?	ဘယ်အရောင်လိုချင်ပါသလဲ be ajaun lou chin ba da le:
size | length	ဆိုဒ် | အရှည် hsou' | ashei
How does it fit?	တော်ရဲ့လား to je. la:
How much is it?	ဒါဘယ်လောက်ကျပါသလဲ da be lau' kja ba dha le:
That's too expensive.	ဒါတော်တော်ဈေးကြီးတယ် da do do zei: gji: de

I'll take it.

ကျွန်ုပ်ဒါယူပါမယ်
kjuhou' da ju ba me

Excuse me, where do I pay?

တဆင့်ဆိတ်လျှောက်ပါ၊
ပိုက်ဆံဘယ်မှာရှင်းရပါမလဲ
ti' hsei' lau' pa/
pai' zan be hma shin: ja. ba ma. le:

Will you pay in cash or credit card?

ဘယ်လိုရှင်းချင်ပါသလဲ၊ ငွေသားနဲ့လား
ကဒ်နဲ့ပါလား
be' lou shin: gjin ba dha le: ngwe dha:
ne. la: ka' ne. ba la:

In cash | with credit card

ငွေသားဖြင့် | ခရက်ဒစ်ကဒ်ဖြင့်
ngwei dha: chin. | kha. ja di' ka' chin.

Do you want the receipt?

ချက်ယူမှာပါလား
che' ju hma ba la:

Yes, please.

ဟုတ်ကဲ့၊ ကောင်းတာပေါ့
hou' ke./ kaun: da bo.

No, it's OK.

ဟုတ်ကဲ့ မလုပ်ပါဘူး
ကျေးဇူးတင်ပါတယ်
hou' ke. ma. lou ba dhu:
kej: zu: din ba de

Thank you. Have a nice day!

ကျေးဇူးတင်ပါတယ်
အစစအရာရာအဆင်ပြေပါစေ
kjei: zu: din ba de
a. za. za. aja ja ahsin bei ba zei

In town

Excuse me, ...	တစ်ဆိတ်လောက်ပါ၊ ကျေးဇူးပြု၍... ti' hsei' lau' pa/ gjei:zu:bju. jwei....
I'm looking for ...	ကျွန်ုပ်...ကိုရှာနေတာပါ kjunou' ... kou'sha nei da. ba
the subway	မီသရို mi' jou
my hotel	ကျွန်ုပ်ဟော်တယ် kjunou' ho te
the movie theater	ရုပ်ရှင်ရုံ jou' shin joun
a taxi stand	တက္ကစီဂိတ် te' kasi gei'

an ATM	အေတီအမ်စက် ei ti. an se'
a foreign exchange office	ငွေလဲဌာန ngwei le: hta. na.
an internet café	အင်တာနက်ကဖေး in ta na' ka. hpei:
... street	...လမ်း ...lan:
this place	ဒီနေရာ di nei ja

Do you know where ... is?	တစ်ဆိတ်လောဘွက်ပါ၊ ...ဘယ်နားမှာရှိလဲသိပါသလား ti' hsei' lau' pa/ ...be na: hma shi. le: dhi. ba dha. la:
Which street is this?	ဒီလမ်းကိုဘယ်လိုခေါ်ပါသလဲ di lan: gou be lou go ba dha le:
Show me where we are right now.	ကျေးဇူးပြု၍ ကျွန်ုပ်တို့အခု ဘယ်မှာလဲဆိုတာ ပြပေးပါ kjei: zu: pju. i. kjun p tou. akhou. be hma le: zou da pja bei: ba
Can I get there on foot?	ကျွန်ုပ်အဲဒီကိုလမ်းလျှောက်သွား လို့ရပါသလား kjunou' e. di gou lan: shau' dhwa: lou. ja. ba dha. la:
Do you have a map of the city?	သင့်ဆီမှာ မြို့မြေပုံရှိပါသလား thin. zi hma mjou. mjei boun shi. ba dha. la:
How much is a ticket to get in?	လက်မှတ်တစ်ဆောင်ဘယ်လောက်ပါလဲ le' hma' ti' hsain be lau' ba le:

Can I take pictures here?

ဒီမှာဓာတ်ပုံရိုက်လို့ရပါသလား
di hma da' poun jai' lou. ja. ba dha la:

Are you open?

ဖွင့်ပါသလား
hpwin. ba dha la:

When do you open?

ဘယ်အချိန်ဖွင့်မှာပါလဲ
be achein bwin. hma ba le:

When do you close?

ဘယ်အချိန်ထိဖွင့်ပါသလဲ
be achein bwin. hma ba da le:

Money

money	ပိုက်ဆံ pai' hsan
cash	လက်ငင်း le' ngin:
paper money	စက္ကူပိုက်ဆံ se' ku bai' hsan
loose change	အကြွေစေ့ akjwei zei.
check | change | tip	ချက် | အကြွေ | ဘောက်ဆူး che' | akjwei | bau' su:
credit card	ခရက်ဒစ်ကဒ် kha. je' di' ka'
wallet	ပိုက်ဆံအိတ် pai' hsan ei'
to buy	ဝယ်သည် we de
to pay	ပေးချေသည် pei: gjei de
fine	ဒဏ်ငွေ dan ngwei
free	အခမဲ့ akha me.
Where can I buy …?	…ကိုဘယ်မှာဝယ်လို့ရပါသလဲ …kou be' hma we' lou. ja ba da le:
Is the bank open now?	အခုဘဏ်ဖွင့်ပါသလား akhu. ban pbwin. ba da la:
When does it open?	အဲ့ဒါဘယ်အချိန်ဖွင့်ပါသလဲ e. da be achein bwin ba dha. le:
When does it close?	အဲ့ဒါဘယ်အချိန်ထိဖွင့်ပါသလဲ e. da be achein hti. bwin ba dha. le:
How much?	ဘယ်လောက်လဲ be lau' le:
How much is this?	ဒါဘယ်လောက်ကျပါသလဲ da be lau' kja ba dha le:
That's too expensive.	ဒါတော်တော်ဈေးကြီးတယ် da do do zei: gji: de
Excuse me, where do I pay?	တစ်ဆိတ်လောက်ပါ၊ ပိုက်ဆံဘယ်မှာရှင်းရပါမလဲ ti' hsei' lau' pa/ pai' zan be hma shin: ja. ba ma. le:

Check, please.

ကျေးဇူးပြု၍ ချက်ပေးပါ
kjei: zu: pju. i. che' bei: ba

Can I pay by credit card?

ခရက်ဒစ်ကဒ်နဲ့ရှင်းလို့ရပါသလား
kha. je' di' ka' he. shin: lou. ja. ba dha. la:

Is there an ATM here?

ဒီမှာအေတီအမ်စက်ရှိပါသလား
di hma ei ti an ze' ba dha la:

I'm looking for an ATM.

ကျွန်ုပ်အေတီအမ်စက်ရှာနေတာပါ
kjuhou' ei ti ein ze' sha hei da ba

I'm looking for a foreign exchange office.

ကျွန်ုပ်ငွေလဲဌာနကိုရှာနေတာပါ
kjuhou' ngwei le: da na gou hja nei da ba

I'd like to change …

ကျွန်ုပ်…လဲချင်လို့ပါ
kjuhou'…le: chin lou. ba

What is the exchange rate?

ငွေလဲနှုန်းကဘယ်လောက်ပါလဲ
ngwei le: hnan: ga. be lau' ba le

Do you need my passport?

ပတ်စပို့ လိုပါသလား
pa's pou. lou ba dha. la:

Time

What time is it?	ဘယ်အချိန်ရှိပြီလဲ be achein shi. bja le:
When?	ဘယ်တော့လဲ be do. le:
At what time?	ဘယ်အချိန်မှာလဲ be achein hma le:
now | later | after ...	အခု | နောက်မှ | ...ပြီးမှ akhu. | nau' hma. |...pji: hma.
one o'clock	နေ့လယ်တစ်နာရီ nei. le di' na ji
one fifteen	တစ်နာရီတစ်ဆယ်ယ်ငါးမိနစ် ti' na ji ti' ze. nga: mi. ni'
one thirty	တစ်နာရီသုံးဆယ်မိနစ် ti' na ji thoun: ze mi. ni'
one forty-five	တစ်နာရီလေးဆယ်ငါးမိနစ် ti' na ji lei:
one | two | three	တစ် | နှစ် | သုံး ti' | hni' | thoun:
four | five | six	လေး | ငါး | ခြောက် lei: | nga: | chau'
seven | eight | nine	ခုနစ် | ရှစ် | ကိုး khun hni' | shi' | kou:
ten | eleven | twelve	တစ်ဆယ် | တစ်ဆယ့်တစ် | တစ်ဆယ့်နှစ် ti' hse | ti' hse. ti' | ti' hse. hni'
in ...	အတွင်း atwin:
five minutes	ငါးမိနစ် nga: mi. ni'
ten minutes	ဆယ်မိနစ် hse mi. ni'
fifteen minutes	ဆယ့်ငါးမိနစ် hse. nga: mi. ni'
twenty minutes	မိနစ်နှစ်ဆယ် mi. ni' hni' ze
half an hour	နာရီဝက် na ji we'
an hour	တစ်နာရီ ti' na ji

in the morning	မနက်ခင်းမှာ
	mane' gin: hma
early in the morning	မနက်စောစော
	mane' so: zo:
this morning	ဒီနေ့မနက်
	di nei. ma. ne'
tomorrow morning	မနက်ဖြန်မနက်
	mane' bjan mane'

in the middle of the day	နေ့လယ်ခင်းမှာ
	nei. le gin: hma
in the afternoon	မွန်းလွဲရှိန်မှာ
	mun: lwe: gjein hma
in the evening	ညနေမှာ
	nja. nei hma
tonight	ဒီည
	di nja

at night	ညမှာ
	nja hma
yesterday	မနေ့က
	ma. nei. ka.
today	ဒီနေ့
	di nei.
tomorrow	မနက်ဖြန်
	mane' bjan
the day after tomorrow	သသက်ခါ
	dhabe' kha

What day is it today?	ဒီနေ့ဘာနေ့လဲ
	di nei. ba nei. le:
It's …	အဲ့ဒါက..
	e. da ga.
Monday	တနလ်ာ
	tanin: la
Tuesday	အင်္ဂါ
	in ga
Wednesday	ဗုဒ္ဓဟူး
	bou da. hu:

Thursday	ကြာသပတေး
	kja dha ba. dei:
Friday	သောကြာ
	thau' kja
Saturday	စနေ
	sanei
Sunday	တနင်္ဂနွေ
	tanin: ganwei

Greetings. Introductions

Hello.
မင်္ဂလာပါ
min ga. la ba

Pleased to meet you.
သိ့ရွင်ရတာဝမ်းသာပါတယ်
thi gwin ja. da wan: dha ba de

Me too.
ကျွန်ုပ်ရောပဲ
kjuhou' jo: be:

I'd like you to meet …
ဒါကတော့…ပါ
da ga. do….ba

Nice to meet you.
တွေ့ရတာ ဝမ်းသာပါတယ်
twei. ja. da wan: dha ba de

How are you?
နေကောင်းပါသလား
nei gaun: ba dha la:

My name is …
ကျွန်ုပ်နာမည်ကတော့…ဖြစ်ပါတယ်
kjuhou' name ka. do….hpi' ba de

His name is …
သူနာမည်ကတော့…ဖြစ်ပါတယ်
thu. name ga do…hpji' ba de

Her name is …
သူမနာမည်ကတော့…ဖြစ်ပါတယ်
thu ma. name ga do….hpji' pa de

What's your name?
သင့်နာမည်ဘယ်လိုခေါ်ပါသလား
thin. name be lou go ba dha la:

What's his name?
သူ့နာမည်ဘယ်လိုခေါ်ပါသလဲ
thu. name be lou kho ba dhale:

What's her name?
သူမနာမည်ဘယ်လိုခေါ်ပါသလဲ
thu ma. name be lou go ba dha le:

What's your last name?
သင့်ရဲ့နောက်ဆုံးနာမည်ကဘာလဲ
thin. je. nau' hsoun: name ga. ba le:

You can call me …
ကျွန်ုပ်ကို…လို့ခေါ်လို့ရပါတယ်
kjuhou' kou'…lou. go lou. ja. ba de

Where are you from?
သင်ကဘယ်ကလဲ
thin ga. be ga. le:

I'm from …
ကျွန်ုပ်က…ကပါ
kjuhou' ka….ka. ba

What do you do for a living?
ဘာအလုပ်လုပ်ပဲ
ba lou' lou' le:

Who is this?
အဲဒါဘယ်သူ့လဲ
e. da be dhu le:

Who is he?
သူကဘယ်သူလဲ
thu ka. be dhu le:

Who is she?
သူမကဘယ်သူ့လဲ
thu ma. ga. be dhu le:

Who are they?
သူတို့ကဘယ်သူတွေလဲ
thu dou. ka. be dhu dwei le:

This is …

ဒါက...ပါ
da ga….ba

my friend (masc.)

ကျွန်ုပ်ရဲ့ သူငယ်ချင်း
kjuhou'je. dhu nge gjin:

my friend (fem.)

ကျွန်ုပ်ရဲ့ မိန်းကလေးသူငယ်ချင်း
kjuhou'je. mein: ga. lei: dhu nge gjin:

my husband

ကျွန်ုပ်ရဲ့ ယောက်ျား
kjuhou'je. jau'kja:

my wife

ကျွန်တော့ရဲ့ မိန်းမ
kjuh do. je: mein: ma.

my father

ကျွန်ုပ်ရဲ့ အဖေ
kjuhou'je. ahpei

my mother

ကျွန်ုပ်ရဲ့ အမေ
kjuhou'je. amei

my brother

ကျွန်ုပ်ရဲ့ အစ်ကိုညီ
kjuhou'je. i' kou/nji

my sister

ကျွန်ုပ်ရဲ့ အစ်မညီမ
kjuhou'je. i' ma./nji ma.

my son

ကျွန်ုပ်ရဲ့ သား
kjuhou'je. dha:

my daughter

ကျွန်ုပ်ရဲ့ သမီး
kjuhou'je. dhami:

This is our son.

ဒါကကျွန်ုပ်တို့ရဲ့ သားပါ
da ga. gjun'p tou. jei. dha: ba

This is our daughter.

ဒါကကျွန်ုပ်တို့ရဲ့ သမီးပါ
da ga. gjun'p tou. jei. thami: ba

These are my children.

ဒါကကျွန်ုပ်ရဲ့ ကလေးတွေပါ
da ga. gjun'p jei. ga. lei: dwei ba

These are our children.

ဒါကကျွန်ုပ်တို့ရဲ့ ကလေးတွေပါ
da ga. gjun'p tou. jei. ga. lei: dwei ba

Farewells

Good bye!
နှုတ်ဆက်ပါတယ်
hnou' hse' pa de

Bye! (inform.)
တာ့တာ
ta. da

See you tomorrow.
မနက်ဖြန်မှ ဆုံကြပါမယ်
mane bjan hmu. zoun gja ba me

See you soon.
နောက်မှ ဆုံကြပါမယ်
nau' hma. zoun gja. ba. me

See you at seven.
ခုနစ်နာရီမှာ ဆုံကြပါမယ်
khun hni na ji hma hsoun gja. ba me

Have fun!
ပျော်ရွှင်ပါစေ
pjo shwin ba zei

Talk to you later.
နောက်မှ ပြောကြပါမယ်
nau' hma. bjo: gja. ba me

Have a nice weekend.
ပျော်ရွှင်သောဝိတ်ရက်ဖြစ်ပါစေ
pjo shwin de. bei je hpji' ba zei

Good night.
ကောင်းသောညပါ
kaun: dho: nja. ba

It's time for me to go.
ကျွန်ုပ်သွားဖို့ အချိန်တန်ပြီ
kjunou thwa: bou. achain dan bji

I have to go.
ကျွန်ုပ်သွားရတော့မယ်
kjunou thwa: ja. do. me

I will be right back.
ကျွန်ုပ်အခုခ ပြန်လာခဲ့ပါမယ်
kjunou' akhou pjan la ge. ba me

It's late.
နောက်ကျနေပြီ
nau' kja. nei bji

I have to get up early.
ကျွန်ုပ်စောစောထရမယ်
kjunou' so: zo: da. ja. me

I'm leaving tomorrow.
ကျွန်ုပ် မနက်ဖြန် ပြန်တော့မယ်
kjunou' ma. ne' hpjan pjan do. me

We're leaving tomorrow.
ကျွန်ုပ်တို့ မနက်ဖြန် ပြန်ကြတော့မယ်
kjunou tou. mane hpjan bjan ga do. me

Have a nice trip!
ပျော်ရွှင်ဖွယ်ခရီးဖြစ်ပါစေ
pjo shin bwe: khaji: hpji' ba zei

It was nice meeting you.
သင်နဲ့ ရင်းနှီးရွင်ရတာ
ဝမ်းသာပါတယ်
thin ne. jin: hni: gwin ja.
da wan: dha ba de

It was nice talking to you.

သင်နဲ့စကားပြောခွင့်ရတာ
ဝမ်းသာပါတယ်
thin nei. zaga: bjo: gwin. ja.
da wan: dha ba de

Thanks for everything.

အစစအရာရာ အတွက် ကျေးဇူးတင်ပါတယ်
a za. za. a ja. ja. atwe' kjei: zu: din ba de

I had a very good time.

ကျွန်ုပ်အတွက်အရမ်းကောင်း
တဲ့အချိန်ဖြစ်ခဲ့ပါတယ်
kjunou' atwe' ajan: kaun:
de. achin hpji' khe. ba de

We had a very good time.

ကျွန်ုပ်တို့အတွက်အရမ်းကောင်း
တဲ့အချိန်ဖြစ်ခဲ့ပါတယ်
kjunou' tou. atwe' ajan: gaun:
de. achein hpji' ge. ba de

It was really great.

ဒါကအရမ်းကောင်းခဲ့ပါတယ်
da ga. ajan: gaun: ge. ba de

I'm going to miss you.

ကျွန်ုပ်လွမ်းနေတော့မှာပဲ
kjunou' lun: nei do. hma be:

We're going to miss you.

ကျွန်ုပ်တို့လွမ်းနေတော့မှာပဲ
kjunou' tou. lun: nei do. hma be:

Good luck!

ကံကောင်းပါစေ
kan gaun: ba zei

Say hi to …

…ကိုမင်္ဂလာပါလို့နှုတ်ဆက်ပေးပါ
…kou nga la ba lou. hnu' ze' pei: ba

Foreign language

I don't understand.	ကျွန်ုပ်နားမလည်ပါဘူး kjunou' na: ma. le ba bu:
Write it down, please.	ကျေးဇူးပြု၍ ရေးပေးပါ kjei: zu: pju. i. jei: bei: ba
Do you speak …?	သင်...လိုပြောတတ်လား thin...lou bjo: da' la:
I speak a little bit of …	ကျွန်ုပ်...လိုနည်းနည်းတော့ပြောတတ်ပါတယ် kjunou'...lou he: ne: to. pjo da' ba de
English	အင်္ဂလိပ် angga. lei'
Turkish	တူရကီ tu ra. ki
Arabic	အာရပ် a ra'
French	ပြင်သစ် pjin dhi'
German	ဂျာမန် gja man
Italian	အီတလီ ita. li
Spanish	စပိန် sapein
Portuguese	ပေါ်တူဂီ po tu gi
Chinese	တရုတ် tajou'
Japanese	ဂျပန် gja pan
Can you repeat that, please.	ကျေးဇူးပြု၍ နောက်တစ်ခေါက်လောက်ပါ kjei: zu: pju. i. nau' ti' la' pa
I understand.	ကျွန်ုပ်နားလည်ပါတယ် kjunou' na: le ba de
I don't understand.	ကျွန်ုပ်နားမလည်ပါဘူး kjunou' na: ma. le ba bu:
Please speak more slowly.	ကျေးဇူးပြု၍ ဖြည်းဖြည်းပြောပေးပါ kjei: zu: pju. i. hpjin: hpjin: pjo: bei: ba
Is that correct? (Am I saying it right?)	ဒါမှန်ပါသလား da hman ba dha la:
What is this? (What does this mean?)	ဒါဘာလဲ da ba le:

Apologies

Excuse me, please.

ကျေးဇူးပြု၍ ခွင့်လွှတ်ပါ
kjei: zu: pju. i. khwin. hla' pa

I'm sorry.

ကျွန်ုပ်စိတ်မကောင်းပါဘူး
kjunou' sei' ma. kaun: ba dhu:

I'm really sorry.

ကျွန်ုပ်တော်တော်စိတ်မကောင်းပါဘူး
kjunou' to do zei' ma gaun: ba bu:

Sorry, it's my fault.

တောင်းပန်ပါတယ် ဒါကကျွန်ုပ်အမှားပါ
thaun: ban ba de da ga. gjun ahma: ba

My mistake.

ကျွန်ုပ်အမှားပါ
kjunou' ahma: ba

May I ...?

ကျွန်ုပ်...လို့ရမလား
kjunou'...lou. ja. ma. la:

Do you mind if I ...?

ကျွန်ုပ်...ရင် သင်စိတ်မဆိုး
ဘူးမလား
kjunou'...jin thin zi' ma. hsou:
dhu: ma. la:

It's OK.

အဆင်ပြေပါတယ်
ahsin bjei ba de

It's all right.

အားလုံးအဆင်ပြေပါတယ်
a: loun: ahsin bjei ba de

Don't worry about it.

အဲဒီအတွက် စိတ်မပူပါနဲ့
e di atwe' sei' ma.bu ba ne.

Agreement

Yes.
ဟုတ်ပါတယ်
hou' pa de

Yes, sure.
ဟုတ်ပါတယ်၊ သေချာပါတယ်
hou' pa de/ thei gja ba de

OK (Good!)
ကောင်းပါတယ်
kain: ba de

Very well.
အရမ်းကောင်းပါတယ်
ajan: gaun: ba de

Certainly!
အသေအရာပဲ
athei acha be:

I agree.
ကျွန်ုပ်သဘောတူပါတယ်
kjuhou' tha bo: du ba de

That's correct.
ဒါမှန်ကန်ပါတယ်
da hman gan ba de

That's right.
ဒါမှန်ပါတယ်
da hman ba de

You're right.
သင်မှန်ပါတယ်
thin hman ba de

I don't mind.
ကျွန်ုပ်စိတ်မရှိပါဘူး
kjuhou' sei' ma. shi. ba dhu:

Absolutely right.
လုံးဝမှန်ကန်ပါတယ်
loun: wa hman gan ba de

It's possible.
ဒါဖြစ်နိုင်ပါတယ်
da bji' nain ba de

That's a good idea.
ဒါအကြံကောင်းပဲ
da akjan gaun: be:

I can't say no.
ကျွန်ုပ် မငြင်းနိုင်ပါဘူး
kjuhou' ma. njin: nain ba dhu:

I'd be happy to.
ဝမ်းသာနေမှာပါ
wan: dha nei hma ba

With pleasure.
ဝမ်းသာအားရစွာ
wan: dha a: jazwa

Refusal. Expressing doubt

No.	မဟုတ်ပါဘူး ma hou' pa bu:
Certainly not.	တကယ်မဟုတ်ပါဘူး dage ma. hou' pa bu:
I don't agree.	ကျွန်ုပ်သဘောမတူပါဘူး kjunou' tha bo: ma. du ba de
I don't think so.	ကျွန်ုပ်တော့ ဒီလိုမထင်ဘူး kjunou' to. di lou ma. din bu:
It's not true.	ဒါမမှန်ဘူး da ma. hman dhu:
You are wrong.	သင်တို့မှားနေပြီ thin dou. hma: nei bji
I think you are wrong.	ကျွန်ုပ်ထင်တာတော့ သင်တို့ မှားနေပြီ kjunou' htin da do. dhin dou. hma: nei bji
I'm not sure.	ကျွန်ုပ်မသေချာဘူး kjunou' ma. dhei gja bu:
It's impossible.	ဒါမဖြစ်နိုင်ဘူး da ma. bji' nain dhu:
Nothing of the kind (sort)!	အဲဒီလိုမျိုး လုံးဝမဟုတ်ဘူး e di lou mjou: loun: wa. ma. hou' bu:
The exact opposite.	အတိအကျကိုပြောင်းပြန် ati. akja. kou pjaun: pjan
I'm against it.	ကျွန်ုပ်ဆန့်ကျင်ပါတယ် kjunou' hsan. kjin ba de
I don't care.	ကျွန်ုပ်ဂရုမစိုက်ပါဘူး kjunou' ga. jou. ma. zai' ba dhu:
I have no idea.	ကျွန်ုပ်မှာအကြံအစည်မရှိဘူး kjunou' hma akjan ase ma. shi. bu:
I doubt it.	ကျွန်ုပ်တော့ဒါကိုသံသယဝင်တယ် kjunou' to. da gou dhan dha. ja. win de
Sorry, I can't.	ခွင့်လွှတ်ပါ၊ ကျွန်ုပ်မတတ်နိုင်ပါဘူး khwin. hlu' pa/ kjun p ma. da nein ba bu:
Sorry, I don't want to.	ခွင့်လွှတ်ပါ၊ ကျွန်ုပ်မလိုချင်ပါဘူး khwin. hlu' pa/ kjun p ma. lou gjin ba bu:
Thank you, but I don't need this.	ကျေးဇူးတင်ပါတယ် ဒါပေမယ့်ကျွန်ုပ်ဒါကိုမလိုပါဘူး kjei: zu: din ba de da bei me. gjunu' da kou ma. lou ba bu:
It's getting late.	နောက်ကျနေပြီ nau' kja. nei bji

I have to get up early.

ကျွန်ုပ်စောစောထရမယ်
kjuṅou' so: zo: da. ja. me

I don't feel well.

ကျွန်ုပ်နေမကောင်းလို့ပါ
kjuṅou' nei ma. kaun: lou. ba

Expressing gratitude

Thank you.

ကျေးဇူးတင်ပါတယ်
kjei: zu: din ba de

Thank you very much.

ကျေးဇူးအများကြီးတင်ပါတယ်
kjei: zu: amja: kji: din ba de

I really appreciate it.

အရမ်းကျေးဇူးတင်ပါတယ်
ajan: gjei: zu: din ba de

I'm really grateful to you.

ကျွန်ုပ်သင့်ကို တကယ်ကို
ကျေးဇူးတင်ပါတယ်
kjunou' thin. kou dage kou
gjei: zu: din ba de

We are really grateful to you.

ကျွန်ုပ်တို့သင့်ကို တွကယ်ကို
ကျေးဇူးတင်ပါတယ်
kjunou' tou. dhin. kou dage kou
gjei: zu: din ba de

Thank you for your time.

အချိန်ပေးတဲ့ အတွက် ကျေးဇူးတင်ပါတယ်
achein bei: de. atwe' kjei: zu: din ba de

Thanks for everything.

အစစအရာရာ အတွက် ကျေးဇူးတင်ပါတယ်
a za. za. a ja. ja. atwe' kjei: zu: din ba de

Thank you for ...

...အတွက် ကျေးဇူးတင်ပါတယ်
...atwe' kjei: zu: din ba de

your help

သင့်ရဲ့ အကူအညီ
thin. je. aku anji

a nice time

ကောင်းသောအချိန်
kaun: dho: achein

a wonderful meal

နှစ်သက်ဖွယ်ကောင်းသောအစားအစာ
hni' the' hpe kaun: dhau asa: asa

a pleasant evening

သာယာကြည်နူးဖွယ်ကောင်း
သောညနေခင်း
tha ja kjei nu: bwe kaun:
dho: nja. nei khan:

a wonderful day

နှစ်သက်ပျော်ရွှင်ဖွယ်ကောင်းသောနေ့
hni' the' pjo shwin bwe gaun: dho: nei.

an amazing journey

စိတ်ဝင်စားစရာကောင်းသောလေ့လာရေးခရီး
sei' win za: zaja gaun: de. lei. la jei: gaji:

Don't mention it.

ရပါတယ်
ja. ba de

You are welcome.

ရပါတယ်
ja. ba de

Any time.

အမြဲတမ်းရပါတယ်
amje: dan: ja ba de

My pleasure.

အကူအညီအတွက်ဝမ်းသာပါတယ်
aku anji atwe' wan dha ba de

Forget it.
ထားလိုက်ပါ အားလုံးအဆင်ပြေပါတယ်
hta: lai' pa a: loun: ahsin bjei ba de

Don't worry about it.
စိတ်မပူပါနဲ့
sei' ma. bu ba ne.

Congratulations. Best wishes

Congratulations!
ဂုဏ်ယူပါတယ်
goun dhu ba de

Happy birthday!
ပျော်ရွှင်စရာမွေးနေ့ဖြစ်ပါစေ
pjo shwin za. ja mwei: nei. hpji' ba zei

Merry Christmas!
မယ်ရီခရစ္စမတ်
me ji'kha. ji' sa. ma'

Happy New Year!
ပျော်ရွှင်ဖွယ်နှစ်သစ်ဖြစ်ပါစေ
pjo shin bwe: hni' thi' hpji' ba zei

Happy Easter!
ဟက်ပီးအီစတာ
he' pi: i sata

Happy Hanukkah!
ဟက်ပီးဟန်နကာ
he' pi: han hu. ka

I'd like to propose a toast.
ကျွန်ုပ်ဆုတောင်းစကားပြောချင်ပါတယ်
kjuhou' hsou daun: zaga: bjo: gjin ba de

Cheers!
ချီးယားစ်
chi: ja: s

Let's drink to …!
…အတွက်သောက်ကြရအောင်
…atwe' thau' kja. ja. aun

To our success!
ကျွန်ုပ်တို့ရဲ့အောင်မြင်မှုအတွက်
kjuhou' tou. je. aun mjin hmu. atwe'

To your success!
သင်တို့ရဲ့အောင်မြင်မှုအတွက်
thin dou. je. aun mjin hmu. atwe'

Good luck!
ကံကောင်းပါစေ
kan gaun: ba zei

Have a nice day!
ကောင်းသောနေ့လေးဖြစ်ပါစေ
kaun: dho: nei. lei: hpji' pa zei

Have a good holiday!
ကောင်းသောအားလပ်ရက်ဖြစ်ပါစေ
kaun: dho: a: la' je' phji' pa zei

Have a safe journey!
လမ်းခရီးမှာအဆင်ပြေပါစေ
lan: khaji: hma ahsin bjei ba zei

I hope you get better soon!
မကြာခင်နေပြန်ကောင်း
ပါစေလို့ဆန္ဒပြုပါတယ်
ma gja. gin nei bjan gaun:
ba zei lou zan da. bju. ba de

Socializing

Why are you sad?	သင်ဘာကြောင့်ဝမ်းနည်းနေတာလဲ thin ba gjaun. wan: ne: nei da le:
Smile! Cheer up!	ပြုံးလိုက်ပါ pjoun: lai' pa
Are you free tonight?	ဒီနေ့ညနေသင်အားမလား di nei. nja nei dhin a: ma. la:
May I offer you a drink?	သင့်ကိုသောက်ဖို့ကမ်းလှမ်း လို့ရမလား thin. gou dhau' bou. gan: hlan: lou. ja. ma. la:
Would you like to dance?	မကချင်ဘူးလား ma. ga gjin dhu: la:
Let's go to the movies.	ရုပ်ရှင်ရုံသွားကြမလား jou' shin dhwa: gja. ma. la:
May I invite you to ...?	...ကိုသွားဖို့သင့်ကိုကမ်း လှမ်းလို့ရမလား ...kou twa: hsou. dhin. kou kan: hlan: lou. ja ma la:
a restaurant	စားသောက်ဆိုင် sa: thau' hsain
the movies	ရုပ်ရှင်ရုံ jou' shin joun
the theater	ကဇာတ်ရုံ ka. za' joun
go for a walk	လမ်းလျှောက်သည် lan: shau' te
At what time?	ဘယ်အချိန်မှာလဲ be achein hma le:
tonight	ဒီည di nja
at six	ခြောက်နာရီမှာ chau' naji hma
at seven	ခုနစ်နာရီမှာ khun hni' na ji hma
at eight	ရှစ်နာရီမှာ shi' na ji hma
at nine	ကိုးနာရီမှာ kou: na ji hma

Do you like it here?	သင်ဒီနေရာမှာကြိုက်လား thin di nei ja hma gjou' la:
Are you here with someone?	သင်ဒီမှာတစ်ယောက်ယောက်နဲ့လား thin di hma di' jau' jau' ne. la:
I'm with my friend.	ကျွန်ုပ်နဲ့သူငယ်ချင်းနဲ့ kjunou' ne. dhu nge gjin: ne.
I'm with my friends.	ကျွန်ုပ်နဲ့သူငယ်ချင်းတွေနဲ့ kjunou' ne. dhu nge gjin: dwei ne.
No, I'm alone.	ကျွန်ုပ်တစ်ယောက်တည်း kjunou' ti' jau' te:

Do you have a boyfriend?	သင့်မှာ ကောင်လေး ရှိလား thin. hma kaun lei: shi. la:
I have a boyfriend.	ကျွန်မမှာ ကောင်လေး ရှိတယ် kjun ma. hma kaun lei: shi. de
Do you have a girlfriend?	သင့်မှာ ကောင်မလေး ရှိလား thin. hma kaun ma lei: shi. la:
I have a girlfriend.	ကျွန်တော်မှာ ကောင်မလေး ရှိတယ် kjun do. hma kaun ma. lei: shi. de

Can I see you again?	ကျွန်ုပ်တို့ထပ်ဆုံကြဦးမလား kjunou' tou da' zoun gja u: ma. la:
Can I call you?	ကျွန်ုပ်သင့်ကိုဖုန်းဆက်လို့ရမလား kjunou' thin. gou hpoun: ze' lou. ja. ma la:
Call me. (Give me a call.)	ကျွန်ုပ်ဆီဖုန်းဆက်ပါ kjunou' zi hpoun: ze' ba
What's your number?	သင့်နံပါတ်ကဘာပါလဲ thin. nan ba t ka. ba ba le:
I miss you.	ကျွန်ုပ်သင့်ကိုလွမ်းပါတယ် kjunou' dhin. kou lun: ba de

You have a beautiful name.	သင့်နာမည်ကအရမ်းလှပါတယ် thin. name ga. ajan: hla. ba de
I love you.	ကျွန်ုပ်သင့်ကိုချစ်တယ် kjunou' thin. kou gji' te
Will you marry me?	သင်ကျွန်ုပ်ကိုလက်ထပ်နိုင်မလား thin gjun p kou le' hta' nain ma la:
You're kidding!	သင်ကနောက်နေတာပဲ thin ga. hau' nei da be:
I'm just kidding.	ကျွန်ုပ် စ နေတာပါ kjunou' za. nei da ba

Are you serious?	အတည်လား ati la:
I'm serious.	အတည်ပါ ati ba
Really?!	တကယ်လား dage la:
It's unbelievable!	ဒါကမယုံနိုင်စရာပဲ da ga. ma. joun nain za. ja be:
I don't believe you.	ကျွန်ုပ်သင့်ကိုမယုံဘူး kjunou' thin. kou ma. joun bu:

I can't.

ကျွန်ုပ်မတတ်နိုင်ပါဘူး
kjuňou' ma. da' nain ba bu:

I don't know.

ကျွန်ုပ်မသိပါဘူး
kjuňou' ma. dhi ba bu:

I don't understand you.

ကျွန်ုပ်သင့်ကိုနားမလည်ဘူး
kjuňou' thin. kou na: ma le bu:

Please go away.

ကျေးဇူးပြု၍ ထွက်သွားပါ
kjei: zu: pju. i. htwei' thwa: ba

Leave me alone!

ကျွန်ုပ်ကိုတစ်ယောက်တည်း ထားခဲ့ပါ
kjuňou' kou di' jau' te: hta: ge. ba

I can't stand him.

ကျွန်ုပ်သူ့ကိုကြည့်လို့မရဘူး
kjuňou' thu. kou kji. lou. ma. ja. bu:

You are disgusting!

သင်ကစိတ်ပျက်စရာကောင်းလိုက်တာ
thin ga. zei' pje' zaja gaun: lai' ta

I'll call the police!

ကျွန်ုပ်ရဲကိုဖုန်းဆက်လိုက်မယ်
kjuňou' je gou hpoun: lai' ze' me

Sharing impressions. Emotions

I like it.	ကျွန်ုပ်ဒါကိုကြိုက်တယ်
	kjuhou' da gou gjou' te
Very nice.	အရမ်းကောင်းတယ်
	ajan: gaun: de
That's great!	ဒါကအရမ်းကောင်းတာပဲ
	da ga. ajan: gaun: da be:
It's not bad.	ဒါကမဆိုးပါဘူး
	ga ga. ma. zou: ba thu.
I don't like it.	ကျွန်ုပ်ဒါကိုမကြိုက်ဘူး
	kjuhou' da gou ma gjou' bu:
It's not good.	ဒါကမကောင်းဘူး
	da ga. ma. gaun: thu:
It's bad.	ဒါကဆိုးတယ်
	da ga. zou: de
It's very bad.	ဒါကအရမ်းဆိုးတယ်
	da ga. ajan: zou: de
It's disgusting.	ဒါကစိတ်ပျက်စရာကောင်းတယ်
	da ga. zi pje' sa. ja gaun: de
I'm happy.	ကျွန်ုပ်ပျော်နေတယ်
	kjuhou' pjo hei de
I'm content.	ကျွန်ုပ်ကျေနပ်နေတယ်
	kjuhou' kjei na' nei de
I'm in love.	ကျွန်ုပ်ချစ်မိနေပြီ
	kjuhou' chi' mi. nei pji
I'm calm.	ကျွန်ုပ်အေးအေးလေးလေးပါပဲ
	kjuhou' ei: ei: hsei: zei: ba be:
I'm bored.	ကျွန်ုပ်ပျင်းနေတယ်
	kjuhou' pjin: nei de
I'm tired.	ကျွန်ုပ်ပင်ပန်းနေတယ်
	kjuhou' pin ban nei de
I'm sad.	ကျွန်ုပ်ဝမ်းနည်းနေတယ်
	kjuhou' wan: ne: nei de
I'm frightened.	ကျွန်ုပ်ထိတ်လန့်နေတယ်
	kjuhou' htei' lan. nei de
I'm angry.	ကျွန်ုပ်ဒေါသထွက်နေတယ်
	kjuhou' do dha dwe' nei de
I'm worried.	ကျွန်ုပ်စိတ်ပူနေတယ်
	kjuhou' sei' pu nei de
I'm nervous.	ကျွန်ုပ်စိတ်လှုပ်ရှားနေတယ်
	kjuhou' sei' lou' sha: nei de

I'm jealous. (envious)　　　ကျွန်ုပ်မနာလိုဖြစ်နေတယ်
kjuhou' ma. na lou bji' nei de

I'm surprised.　　　　　　ကျွန်ုပ်အံ့အားသင့်နေတယ်
kjuhou' an. a: dhin. nei de

I'm perplexed.　　　　　　ကျွန်ုပ်စိတ်ရှုပ်နေတယ်
kjuhou' sei' shou' nei de

Problems. Accidents

I've got a problem.	ကျွန်ုပ်မှာအခက်အခဲရှိနေတယ် kjunou' hma akha' akhe: shi. nei de
We've got a problem.	ကျွန်ုပ်တို့မှာ အခက်အခဲရှိနေတယ် kjunou' tou. akha' akhe: shi. nei de
I'm lost.	ကျွန်ုပ်လမ်းပျောက်ခဲ့တယ် kjunou' lan: pjau' khe. de
I missed the last bus (train).	ကျွန်ုပ်နောက်ဆုံးဘတ်စ်ကား ကိုမမီခဲ့ဘူး kjunou' nau' zoun: ba's ka: kou ma. mi ge. bu:
I don't have any money left.	ကျွန်ုပ်မှာပိုက်ဆံလုံး ဝမကျန်တော့ဘူး kjunou' hma bou' zan lou: wa. ma. kjan do. bu:
I've lost my ...	ကျွန်ုပ်...ပျောက်ခဲ့တယ် kjunou'...pjau' khe. de
Someone stole my ...	ကျွန်ုပ်ရဲ့...အခိုးခံလိုက်ရတယ် kjunou' je....akhou: gan lai' ja. de
passport	ပတ်စ်ပို့ pa's pou.
wallet	ပိုက်ဆံအိတ် pai' hsan ei'
papers	စာရွက်စာတမ်း sajwe' zatan:
ticket	လက်မှတ် le' hma'
money	ပိုက်ဆံ pai' hsan
handbag	လက်ကိုင်အိတ် le' kain ei'
camera	ကင်မရာ kin ma. ja
laptop	လပ်တော့ပ် la' to. p
tablet computer	တပ်ဘလက် ta' bale'
mobile phone	မိုဘိုင်းဖုန်း mou bain: boun:
Help me!	ကူညီပါ ku nji ba
What's happened?	ဘာဖြစ်တာလဲ ba bji' ta le:

fire	မီး mi:
shooting	ပစ်ခတ်မှု pi' che' hmu.
murder	လူသတ်မှု lu dha' hmu.
explosion	ပေါက်ကွဲမှု pau' kwe: hmu.
fight	တိုက်ခိုက်မှု tai' khai' hmu.
Call the police!	ရဲကိုခေါ်ပေးပါ je: gou go bei: ba
Please hurry up!	ကျေးဇူးပြု၍မြန်မြန်လုပ်ပေးပါ kjei: zu: pju. i. mjan mjan lou' pei: ba
I'm looking for the police station.	ကျွန်ုပ်ရဲစခန်းကိုရှာနေတာပါ kjunou' je zakhan: kou sha nei da ba
I need to make a call.	ကျွန်ုပ်ဖုန်းဆက်ဖို့လိုတယ် kjunou' hpoun: ze' hpou. lou de
May I use your phone?	ကျွန်ုပ် ခင်ဗျားရဲ့ဖုန်း ဆက်လို့ရမလား kjunou' khin bja: je. hpoun: hse' lou. ja. ma. la:

I've been ...	ကျွန်ုပ်ကို... kjunou' kou…
mugged	ရိုက်နက်လုယက်သွားကြတယ် jou' hne' lu. je' thwa: gja. de
robbed	ဓားပြတိုက်သွားကြတယ် damja. tai' dhwa: gja de
raped	မုဒိန်းကျင့်သွားကြတယ် mu. dein: gjin. dhwa: gja de
attacked (beaten up)	ရိုက်နက်သွားကြတယ် jou' hne' thwa: gja de

Are you all right?	အဆင်ပြေလား ahsin bjei la:
Did you see who it was?	ဘယ်သူလဲဆိုတာသင်မြင်ခဲ့လား be dhu le: zou da dhin mjin gei. la:
Would you be able to recognize the person?	သင်သူ့ကိုမှတ်မိနိုင်မလား thin dhu. gou hma' mi. nein ma. la:
Are you sure?	သင်သေချာရဲ့လား thin dhei gja je. la:
Please calm down.	စိတ်အေးအေးထားပါ sei' ei: ei: da: ba
Take it easy!	အေးအေးဆေးဆေးနေပါ ei: ei: hsei: zei: nei ba
Don't worry!	စိတ်မပူပါနဲ့ sei' ma. bu ba ne.
Everything will be fine.	အားလုံးအဆင်ပြေမှာပါ a: louh: ahsin bjei hma ba
Everything's all right.	အားလုံးအဆင်ပြေပါတယ် a: louh: ahsin bjei ba de

Come here, please.	ကျေးဇူးပြု၍ ဒီကိုလာခဲ့ပါ kjei: zu: pju. i. di kou la ge. ba
I have some questions for you.	ကျွန်ုပ်သင့်ကိုမေးခွန်းနည်း နည်းမေးစရာရှိတယ် kjunou' thin. kou mei: gwan: ne: mei: zaja shi. de
Wait a moment, please.	ကျေးဇူးပြု၍ စောင့်ပေးပါ kjei: zu: pju. i. hsaun. bei: ba
Do you have any I.D.?	သင့်မှာ စာရွက်စာတမ်းရှိပါသလား thin. hma za jwe' sa tan: shi. ba dha. la:
Thanks. You can leave now.	ကျေးဇူးတင်ပါတယ်၊သင်သွားလို့ရပါပြီ kjei: zu: din ba de thin thwa: lou. ja. ba bji
Hands behind your head!	လက်ကိုခေါင်းနောက်မှာထားပါ le' kou khaun: nau' hma hta: ba
You're under arrest!	သင့်ကိုဖမ်းထားပြီ thin. gou ban: da: bji

Health problems

Please help me.	ကျေးဇူးပြု၍ ကျွန်ုပ်ကိုကူညီပါ kjei: zu: pju. r. kjun p kou: ku nji ba
I don't feel well.	ကျွန်ုပ်နေမကောင်းလို့ပါ kjunou'nei ma. kaun: lou. ba
My husband doesn't feel well.	ကျွန်ုပ်မယောက်ျားနေမကောင်းလို့ပါ kjun ma. jau kja: nei ma. kaun: lou. ba
My son ...	ကျွန်ုပ်ရဲ့သား... kjunou' je. dha:...
My father ...	ကျွန်ုပ်ရဲ့အဖေ... kjunou' je. ahpei...

My wife doesn't feel well.	ကျွန်တော့ရဲ့ ဇနီးမနေမ ကောင်းလို့ပါ kjun do. je: mein: ma. nei ma. kaun: lou. ba
My daughter ...	ကျွန်ုပ်သမီး... kjunou' thami:
My mother ...	ကျွန်ုပ်အမေ... kjunou' amei...

I've got a ...	ကျွန်ုပ်... kjunou'...
headache	ခေါင်းကိုက်နေပါတယ် gaun: kai' nei ba de
sore throat	လည်ချောင်းနာနေပါတယ် le gjaun: na nei ba de
stomach ache	ဗိုက်အောင့်နေပါတယ် bai' aun. nei ba de
toothache	သွားကိုက်နေပါတယ် thwa: kai' nei ba de

I feel dizzy.	ကျွန်ုပ်ခေါင်းမူးနေပါတယ် kjunou' gaun: mu: nei ba de
He has a fever.	သူဖျားနေတယ် thu bja: nei de
She has a fever.	သူမဖျားနေတယ် thu ma. bja: nei de
I can't breathe.	ကျွန်ုပ်အသက်မရှူနိုင်ဘူး kjunou' athe' ma. shu nain dhu:

| I'm short of breath. | ကျွန်ုပ် အသက်ရှူကျပ်နေတယ်
kjunou' athe' shu kji' nei de |
| I am asthmatic. | ကျွန်ုပ်က ရင်ကျပ်ဝေဒနာသည်ပါ
kjunou' ka. jin kja' wei da. na de ba |

I am diabetic.	ကျွန်ုပ်က ဆီးချိုဝေဒနာသည်ပါ kjunou' ka. ji: gjou wei da. na de ba
I can't sleep.	ကျွန်ုပ် အိပ်မပျော်ဘူးဖြစ်နေတယ် kjunou' ei' ma. pjo dhu hpji' nei de
food poisoning	အစာအဆိပ်သင့်ခြင်း asa: ahsei' thin. gjin:

It hurts here.	ဒီမှာနာနေတယ် di hma na nei de
Help me!	ကူညီပါ ku nji ba
I am here!	ကျွန်ုပ်ဒီမှာပါ kjunou' di hma ba
We are here!	ကျွန်ုပ်တို့ဒီမှာပါ kjunou' tou. di hma ba
Get me out of here!	ကျွန်ုပ်ကိုဒီကဆွဲထုတ်ပေးပါ kjunou' kou di ka. hswe: htou' bei: ba
I need a doctor.	ကျွန်ုပ်ဆရာဝန်လိုတယ် kjunou' hsaja wun lou de
I can't move.	ကျွန်ုပ်လှုပ်လို့မရဘူး kjunou' hla' lou. ma. ja. thu:
I can't move my legs.	ကျွန်ုပ်ခြေထောက်မရှိ သလိုခံစားရတယ် kjunou' khei dau' ma shi. dha. lou khan za: ja. de

I have a wound.	ကျွန်ုပ်ဒဏ်ရာရထားတယ် kjunou' dan ja ja. da: de
Is it serious?	ပြင်းထန်လား pjin: dan la:
My documents are in my pocket.	ကျွန်ုပ်ရဲ့စာရွက်စာတမ်း တွေအိတ်ကပ်ထဲမှာရှိပါတယ် kjunou' je. zazwe' sa dan: dwei ei' ka' hma shi. ba de
Calm down!	စိတ်အေးအေးထားပါ sei' ei: ei: da: ba
May I use your phone?	ကျွန်ုပ်ဖုန်းဆက်လို့ရမလား kjunou' hpoun: ze' lou. ja. ma. la:

Call an ambulance!	လူနာတင်ကားခေါ်ပေးပါ lu na din ga: go bei: ba
It's urgent!	အမြန် aman
It's an emergency!	အမြန်ဆုံး aman zoun:
Please hurry up!	ကျေးဇူးပြု၍မြန်မြန်လုပ်ပေးပါ kjei: zu: pju. i. mjan mjan lou' pei: ba
Would you please call a doctor?	ကျေးဇူးပြု၍ ဆရာဝန်ခေါ်ပေးပါ kjei: zu: pju. i. hsaja. wun go bei: ba
Where is the hospital?	ဆေးရုံဘယ်နားမှာပါလဲ hsei: joun be na: hma ba le:

How are you feeling?	သင်ဘယ်လိုခံစားနေရလဲ thin be lou gan za: nei ja. le
Are you all right?	အဆင်ပြေလား ahsin bjei la:
What's happened?	ဘာဖြစ်တာလဲ ba bji' ta le:
I feel better now.	ကျွန်ုပ်သက်သာလာပြီ kjunou' the' dha la pji
It's OK.	အားလုံးအဆင်ပြေပါတယ် a: loun: ahsin bjei ba de
It's all right.	အားလုံးအဆင်ပြေပါတယ် a: loun: ahsin bjei ba de

At the pharmacy

pharmacy (drugstore)
ဆေးဆိုင်
hsei: zain

24-hour pharmacy
၂၄ နာရီဆေးဆိုင်
hna hse. lei: ha ji zei:

Where is the closest pharmacy?
အနီးဆုံးဆေးဆိုင်ဘယ်နား မှာရှိပါသလဲ
ani: zoun: zei: zein: be na: hma shi. ba dha le:

Is it open now?
အဲ့ဒါအခုဖွင့်လား
e. da akhu. bwin la:

At what time does it open?
အဲ့ဒါဘယ်အချိန်ဖွင့်ပါသလဲ
e. da be achein bwin ba dha. le:

At what time does it close?
အဲ့ဒါဘယ်အချိန်ထိဖွင့်ပါသလဲ
e. da be achein hti. bwin ba dha. le:

Is it far?
အဲ့ဒါဝေးလား
e. da wei: la:

Can I get there on foot?
ကျွန်ုပ်အဲ့ဒီကိုလမ်းလျှောက်သွား လို့ရပါသလား
kjunou' e. di gou lan: shau' dhwa: lou. ja. ba dha. la:

Can you show me on the map?
ကျေးဇူးပြု၍ ကျွန်ုပ်ကိုမြေပုံပေါ်မှာ ပြပေးပါလား
kjei: zu: pju. i. kjun p kou:

Please give me something for …
ကျွန်ုပ်ကို...ပျောက်ဆေးပေးပါ
kjunou' kou…pjau' hsei: bei: ba:

a headache
ခေါင်းကိုက်
gaun: kai'

a cough
ချောင်းဆိုး
gaun: zou:

a cold
အအေးမိ
aei: mi.

the flu
တုပ်ကွေး
tou' kwei:

a fever
အဖျား
ahpja:

a stomach ache
အစာအိမ်နာ
asa: ein na

nausea
ပျို့အန်
pjou. an

diarrhea
ဝမ်းလျှော
wan: sho:

constipation	ဝမ်းချုပ် wan: gjou'
pain in the back	ကျောအောင့်ခြင်း kjo: aun. gjin:
chest pain	ရင်ဘတ်အောင့်ခြင်း jin ba' aun. gjin:
side stitch	ဘေးအောင့်ခြင်း bei: aun. gjin:
abdominal pain	ဗိုက်အောင့်ခြင်း bai' aun. gjin:

pill	ဆေးပြား hsei: bja:
ointment, cream	ကရင်မ် ka. jin m
syrup	ဆေးရည် hsei: ji:
spray	စပရေး sa. pa. rei
drops	အစက်ချဆေး ase' cha. hsei:

You need to go to the hospital.	သင်ဆေးရုံသွားဖို့လိုတယ် thin zei: joun thwa: bou. lou de
health insurance	ကျန်းမာရေး အာမခံ kjan: ma jei: ama. gan
prescription	ဆေးညွှန်း hsei: hnjun:
insect repellant	ပိုးသတ်ဆေး pou: dha' zei:
Band Aid	ပလာစတာ pa. la sata

The bare minimum

Excuse me, …	တစ်ဆိတ်လောက်ပါ... ti' hsei' lau' pa…
Hello.	မင်္ဂလာပါ min ga. la ba
Thank you.	ကျေးဇူးတင်ပါတယ် kjei: zu: din ba de
Good bye.	နှုတ်ဆက်ပါတယ် hnou' hse' pa de
Yes.	ဟုတ်ပါတယ် hou' pa de
No.	မဟုတ်ပါဘူး ma hou' pa bu:
I don't know.	ကျွန်ုပ်မသိပါဘူး kjunou' ma. dhi ba bu:
Where? | Where to? | When?	ဘယ်မှာလဲ | ဘယ်ကိုလဲ | ဘယ်တော့လဲ be hma le: | be gou le: | be dau. le:

I need …	ကျွန်ုပ်...လိုအပ်တယ် kjunou'…lou a' te
I want …	ကျွန်ုပ်...လိုချင်တယ် kjunou'…lou gjin de
Do you have ...?	သင့်မှာ...ရှိပါသလား thin. hma…shi. ba dha. la:
Is there a … here?	ဒီမှာ...ရှိပါသလား di hma…shi. ba dha la:
May I …?	ကျွန်ုပ်...လို့ရမလား kjunou'…lou. ja. ma. la:
…, please (polite request)	ကျေးဇူးပြု၍... kjei: zu: pju. i….

I'm looking for …	ကျွန်ုပ်...ကိုရှာနေတာပါ kjunou' ... kou sha nei da. ba
the restroom	အိမ်သာ ein dha
an ATM	အေတီအမ်စက် ei ti. an se'
a pharmacy (drugstore)	ဆေးဆိုင် hsei: zain
a hospital	ဆေးရုံ hsei: joun
the police station	ရဲစခန်း je: za. gan:
the subway	မီထရို mi' jou

a taxi	တက္ကစီ te' kasi
the train station	ရထားဘူတာရုံ jatha: buda joun

My name is …	ကျွန်ုပ်နာမည်ကတော့...ဖြစ်ပါတယ် kjuhou' name ka. do....hpi' ba de
What's your name?	သင့်နာမည်ဘယ်လိုခေါ်ပါသလဲ thin.' name be lou go ba dha la:
Could you please help me?	ကျေးဇူးပြု၍ ကျွန်ုပ်ကိုကူညီနိုင်မလား kjei: zu: pju. i. kjun p kou: ku nji nain ma. la:
I've got a problem.	ကျွန်ုပ်မှာအခက်အခဲရှိနေတယ် kjuhou' hma akha' akhe: shi. nei de
I don't feel well.	ကျွန်ုပ်နေမကောင်းပါ kjuhou' nei ma. kaun: ba
Call an ambulance!	လူနာတင်ကားခေါ်ပေးပါ lu na din ga: go bei: ba
May I make a call?	ကျွန်ုပ်ဖုန်းဆက်လို့ရမလား kjuhou' hpoun: ze' lou. ja. ma. la:

I'm sorry.	တောင်းပန်ပါတယ် thaun: ban ba de
You're welcome.	ရပါတယ် ja. ba de

I, me	ကျွန်ုပ် kjuhou'
you (inform.)	သင် thin
he	သူ thu
she	သူမ thu ma.
they (masc.)	သူတို့ thu dou.
they (fem.)	သူမတို့ thu ma. dou.
we	ကျွန်ုပ်တို့ kjuhou' tou.
you (pl)	သင်တို့ thin dou.
you (sg, form.)	သင် thin

ENTRANCE	အဝင် awin
EXIT	အထွက် a htwe'
OUT OF ORDER	အလုပ်မလုပ်ပါ alou' ma lou' pa

CLOSED   ပိတ်သည်
pei' te

OPEN   ဖွင့်သည်
hpwin. de

FOR WOMEN   အမျိုးသမီးများအတွက်
amjou: dhami: mja: atwe'

FOR MEN   အမျိုးသားများအတွက်
amjou: dha: mja: atwe'

MINI DICTIONARY

This section contains 250 useful words required for everyday communication. You will find the names of months and days of the week here. The dictionary also contains topics such as colors, measurements, family, and more

T&P Books Publishing

DICTIONARY CONTENTS

T&P Books Publishing

time	အချိန်	achein
hour	နာရီ	na ji
half an hour	နာရီဝက်	na ji we'
minute	မိနစ်	mi. ni'
second	စက္ကန့်	se' kan.
today (adv)	ယနေ့	ja. nei.
tomorrow (adv)	မနက်ဖြန်	mane' bjan
yesterday (adv)	မနေ့က	ma. nei. ka.
Monday	တနင်္လာ	tanin: la
Tuesday	အင်္ဂါ	in ga
Wednesday	ဗုဒ္ဓဟူး	bou' da. hu:
Thursday	ကြာသပတေး	kja dha ba. dei:
Friday	သောကြာ	thau' kja
Saturday	စနေ	sanei
Sunday	တနင်္ဂနွေ	tanin: ganwei
day	နေ့	nei.
working day	ရုံးဖွင့်ရက်	joun: hpwin je'
public holiday	ပွဲတော်ရက်	pwe: do je'
weekend	ရုံးပိတ်ရက်များ	joun: hpwin je' mja:
week	ရက်သတ္တပတ်	je' tha' daba'
last week (adv)	ပြီးခဲ့တဲ့အပတ်က	pji: ge. de. apa' ka.
next week (adv)	လာမယ့်အပတ်မှာ	la. me. apa' hma
in the morning	နံနက်ခင်းမှာ	nan ne' gin: hma
in the afternoon	နေ့လယ်စာစားချိန်ပြီးနောက်	nei. le za za: gjein bji: nau'
in the evening	ညနေခင်းမှာ	nja. nei gin: hma
tonight (this evening)	ယနေ့ညနေ	ja. nei. nja. nei
at night	ညမှာ	nja hma
midnight	သန်းခေါင်ယံ	than: gaun jan
January	ဇန်နဝါရီလ	zan na. wa ji la.
February	ဖေဖော်ဝါရီလ	hpei bo wa ji la
March	မတ်လ	ma' la.
April	ဧပြီလ	ei bji la.
May	မေလ	mei la.
June	ဇွန်လ	zun la.
July	ဇူလိုင်လ	zu lain la.
August	သြဂုတ်လ	o: gou' la.

73

September	စက်တင်ဘာလ	sa' htin ba la.
October	အောက်တိုဘာလ	au' tou ba la
November	နိုဝင်ဘာလ	nou win ba la.
December	ဒီဇင်ဘာလ	di zin ba la.
in spring	နွေဦးရာသီမှာ	nwei u: ja dhi hma
in summer	နွေရာသီမှာ	nwei ja dhi hma
in fall	ဆောင်းဦးရာသီမှာ	hsaun: u: ja dhi hma
in winter	ဆောင်းရာသီမှာ	hsaun: ja dhi hma
month	လ	la.
season (summer, etc.)	ရာသီ	ja dhi
year	နှစ်	hni'

2. Numbers. Numerals

0 zero	သုည	thoun nja.
1 one	တစ်	ti'
2 two	နှစ်	hni'
3 three	သုံး	thoun:
4 four	လေး	lei:
5 five	ငါး	nga:
6 six	ခြောက်	chau'
7 seven	ခုနှစ်	khun hni'
8 eight	ရှစ်	shi'
9 nine	ကိုး	kou:
10 ten	တစ်ဆယ်	ti' hse
11 eleven	တစ်ဆယ့်တစ်	ti' hse. ti'
12 twelve	တစ်ဆယ့်နှစ်	ti' hse. hni'
13 thirteen	တစ်ဆယ့်သုံး	ti' hse. thoun:
14 fourteen	တစ်ဆယ့်လေး	ti' hse. lei:
15 fifteen	တစ်ဆယ့်ငါး	ti' hse. nga:
16 sixteen	တစ်ဆယ့်ခြောက်	ti' hse. khau'
17 seventeen	တစ်ဆယ့်ခုနှစ်	ti' hse. khu ni'
18 eighteen	တစ်ဆယ့်ရှစ်	ti' hse. shi'
19 nineteen	တစ်ဆယ့်ကိုး	ti' hse. gou:
20 twenty	နှစ်ဆယ်	hni' hse
30 thirty	သုံးဆယ်	thoun: ze
40 forty	လေးဆယ်	lei: hse
50 fifty	ငါးဆယ်	nga: ze
60 sixty	ခြောက်ဆယ်	chau' hse
70 seventy	ခုနှစ်ဆယ်	khun hni' hse.
80 eighty	ရှစ်ဆယ်	shi' hse
90 ninety	ကိုးဆယ်	kou: hse
100 one hundred	တစ်ရာ	ti' ja

200 two hundred	နှစ်ရာ	hni' ja
300 three hundred	သုံးရာ	thoun: ja
400 four hundred	လေးရာ	lei: ja
500 five hundred	ငါးရာ	nga: ja
600 six hundred	ခြောက်ရာ	chau' ja
700 seven hundred	ခုနစ်ရာ	khun hni' ja
800 eight hundred	ရှစ်ရာ	shi' ja
900 nine hundred	ကိုးရာ	kou: ja
1000 one thousand	တစ်ထောင်	ti' htaun
10000 ten thousand	တစ်သောင်း	ti' thaun:
one hundred thousand	တစ်သိန်း	ti' thein:
million	တစ်သန်း	ti' than:
billion	ဘီလီယံ	bi li jan

3. Humans. Family

man (adult male)	အမျိုးသား	amjou: dha:
young man	လူငယ်	lu nge
woman	အမျိုးသမီး	amjou: dhami:
girl (young woman)	မိန်းကလေး	mein: ga. lei:
old man	လူကြီး	lu gji:
old woman	အမျိုးသမီးကြီး	amjou: dhami: gji:
mother	အမေ	amei
father	အဖေ	ahpei
son	သား	tha:
daughter	သမီး	thami:
brother	ညီအစ်ကို	nji a' kou
sister	ညီအစ်မ	nji a' ma
parents	မိဘတွေ	mi. ba. dwei
child	ကလေး	kalei:
children	ကလေးများ	kalei: mja:
stepmother	မိထွေး	mi. dwei:
stepfather	ပထွေး	pahtwei:
grandmother	အဘွား	ahpwa
grandfather	အဘိုး	ahpou:
grandson	မြေး	mjei:
granddaughter	မြေးမ	mjei: ma.
grandchildren	မြေးများ	mjei: mja:
uncle	ဦးလေး	u: lei:
aunt	အဒေါ်	ado
nephew	တူ	tu
niece	တူမ	tu ma.
wife	မိန်းမ	mein: ma.

husband	ယောက်ျား	jau' kja:
married (masc.)	မိန်းမရှိသော	mein: ma. shi. de.
married (fem.)	ယောက်ျားရှိသော	jau' kja: shi de
widow	မုဆိုးမ	mu. zou: ma.
widower	မုဆိုးဖို	mu. zou: bou

name (first name)	အမည်	amji
surname (last name)	မိသားစုအမည်	mi. dha: zu. amji

relative	ဆွေမျိုး	hswe mjou:
friend (masc.)	သူငယ်ချင်း	thu nge gjin:
friendship	ခင်မင်ရင်းနှီးမှု	khin min jin: ni: hmu.

partner	လုပ်ဖော်ကိုင်ဖက်	lou' hpo kain be'
superior (n)	အထက်လူကြီး	a hte' lu gji:
colleague	လုပ်ဖော်ကိုင်ဖက်	lou' hpo kain be'
neighbors	အိမ်နီးနားချင်းများ	ein ni: na: gjin: mja:

4. Human body

body	ခန္ဓာကိုယ်	khan da kou
heart	နှလုံး	hnaloun:
blood	သွေး	thwei:
brain	ဦးနောက်	oun: hnau'

bone	အရိုး	ajou:
spine (backbone)	ကျောရိုး	kjo: jou:
rib	နံရိုး	nan jou:
lungs	အဆုတ်	ahsou'
skin	အရေပြား	ajei bja:

head	ခေါင်း	gaun:
face	မျက်နှာ	mje' hna
nose	နှာခေါင်း	hna gaun:
forehead	နဖူး	na. hpu:
cheek	ပါး	pa:

mouth	ပါးစပ်	pa: zi'
tongue	လျှာ	sha
tooth	သွား	thwa:
lips	နှုတ်ခမ်း	hna' khan:
chin	မေးစေ့	mei: zei.

ear	နားရွက်	na: jwe'
neck	လည်ပင်း	le bin:
eye	မျက်စိ	mje' si.
pupil	သူငယ်အိမ်	thu nge ein
eyebrow	မျက်ခုံး	mje' khoun:
eyelash	မျက်တောင်	mje' taun
hair	ဆံပင်	zabin

hairstyle	ဆံပင်ပုံစံ	zabin boun zan
mustache	နှုတ်ခမ်းမွေး	hnou' khan: hmwei:
beard	မုတ်ဆိတ်မွေး	mou' hsei' hmwei:
to have (a beard, etc.)	အရှည်ထားသည်	ashei hta: de
bald (adj)	ထိပ်ပြောင်သော	htei' pjaun de.

hand	လက်	le'
arm	လက်မောင်း	le' maun:
finger	လက်ချောင်း	le' chaun:
nail	လက်သည်းခွံ	le' the: dou' tan zin:
palm	လက်ဝါး	le' wa:

shoulder	ပခုံး	pakhoun:
leg	ခြေထောက်	chei htau'
knee	ဒူး	du:
heel	ခြေဖနောင့်	chei ba. naun.
back	ကျော	kjo:

5. Clothing. Personal accessories

clothes	အဝတ်အစား	awu' aza:
coat (overcoat)	ကုတ်အကျီရှည်	kou' akji shi
fur coat	သားမွေးအနွေးထည်	tha: mwei: anwei: de
jacket (e.g., leather ~)	အပေါ်အကျီ	apo akji.
raincoat (trenchcoat, etc.)	မိုးကာအကျီ	mou: ga akji

shirt (button shirt)	ရှပ်အကျီ	sha' in gji
pants	ဘောင်းဘီ	baun: bi
suit jacket	အပေါ်အကျီ	apo akji.
suit	အနောက်တိုင်းဝတ်စုံ	anau' tain: wu' saun

dress (frock)	ဂါဝန်	ga wun
skirt	စကတ်	saka'
T-shirt	တီရှပ်	ti shi'
bathrobe	ရေချိုးခန်းဝတ်စုံ	jei gjou: gan: wu' soun
pajamas	ညအိပ်ဝတ်စုံ	nja a' wu' soun
workwear	အလုပ်ဝင်ဝတ်စုံ	alou' win wu' zoun

underwear	အတွင်းခံ	atwin: gan
socks	ခြေအိတ်များ	chei ei' mja:
bra	ဘရာစီယာ	ba ra si ja
pantyhose	အသားကပ်-ဘောင်းဘီရှည်	atha: ka' baun: bi shei
stockings (thigh highs)	စတော့ကင်	sato. kin
bathing suit	ရေကူးဝတ်စုံ	jei ku: wa' zoun

hat	ဦးထုပ်	u: htou'
footwear	ဖိနပ်	hpana'
boots (e.g., cowboy ~)	လည်ရှည်ဖိနပ်	le she bi. na'
heel	ဒေါက်	dau'
shoestring	ဖိနပ်ကြိုး	hpana' kjou:

shoe polish	ဖိနပ်တိုက်ဆေး	hpana' tou' hsei:
gloves	လက်အိတ်	lei' ei'
mittens	နှစ်ကန့်လက်အိတ်	hni' kan. le' ei'
scarf (muffler)	မာဖလာ	ma ba. la
glasses (eyeglasses)	မျက်မှန်	mje' hman
umbrella	ထီး	hti:

tie (necktie)	လည်စည်း	le zi:
handkerchief	လက်ကိုင်ပုဝါ	le' kain bu. wa
comb	ဘီး	bi:
hairbrush	ခေါင်းဘီး	gaun: bi:

buckle	ခါးပတ်ခေါင်း	kha: ba' khaun:
belt	ခါးပတ်	kha: ba'
purse	မိန်းကလေးပုခုံး လွယ်အိတ်	mein: galei: bou goun: lwe ei'

6. House. Apartment

apartment	တိုက်ခန်း	tai' khan:
room	အခန်း	akhan:
bedroom	အိပ်ခန်း	ei' khan:
dining room	ထမင်းစားခန်း	htamin: za: gan:

living room	ဧည့်ခန်း	e. gan:
study (home office)	အိမ်တွင်းရုံးခန်းလေး	ein dwin: joun: gan: lei:
entry room	ဝင်ပေါက်	win bau'
bathroom (room with a bath or shower)	ရေချိုးခန်း	jei gjou gan:
half bath	အိမ်သာ	ein dha

vacuum cleaner	ဖုန်စုပ်စက်	hpoun zou' se'
mop	လက်ကိုင်ရှည်ကြမ်း သုတ်ဖတ်	le' kain she gjan: dhou' hpa'
dust cloth	ဖုန်သုတ်အဝတ်	hpoun dou' awu'
short broom	တံမြက်စည်း	tan mje' si:
dustpan	အမှိုက်ဂေါ်	ahmai' go

furniture	ပရိဘောဂ	pa ri. bo: ga.
table	စားပွဲ	sa: bwe:
chair	ကုလားထိုင်	kala: dain
armchair	လက်တင်ပါသောကုလားထိုင်	le' tin ba dho: ku. la: dain

mirror	မှန်	hman
carpet	ကော်ဇော	ko zo:
fireplace	မီးလင်းဖို	mi: lin: bou
drapes	ခန်းဆီးရှည်	khan: zi: shei
table lamp	စားပွဲတင်မီးအိမ်	sa: bwe: din mi: ein
chandelier	မီးပန်းဆိုင်း	mi: ban: zain:
kitchen	မီးဖိုခန်း	mi: bou gan:

gas stove (range)	ဂတ်စ်မီးဖို	ga' s mi: bou
electric stove	လျှပ်စစ်မီးဖို	hlja' si' si: bou
microwave oven	မိုက်ခရိုဝေ့ဗ်	mou' kha. jou wei. b

refrigerator	ရေခဲသေတ္တာ	je ge: dhi' ta
freezer	ရေခဲခန်း	jei ge: gan:
dishwasher	ပန်းကန်ဆေးစက်	bagan: zei: ze'
faucet	ရေပိုက်ခေါင်း	jei bai' khaun:

meat grinder	အသားကြိတ်စက်	atha: kjei' za'
juicer	အသီးဖျော်စက်	athi: hpjo ze'
toaster	ပေါင်မုန့်ကင်စက်	paun moun. gin ze'
mixer	မွှေစက်	hmwei ze'

coffee machine	ကော်ဖီဖျော်စက်	ko hpi hpjo ze'
kettle	ရေနွေးကရားအိုး	jei nwei: gaja: ou:
teapot	လက်ဘက်ရည်အိုး	le' be' ji ou:

TV set	ရုပ်မြင်သံကြားစက်	jou' mjin dhan gja: ze'
VCR (video recorder)	ဗီဒီယိုပြစက်	bi di jou bja. ze'
iron (e.g., steam ~)	မီးပူ	mi: bu
telephone	တယ်လီဖုန်း	te li hpoun: